Ladrica Menson-Furr

D1360411

August Wilson's
Fences

continuum

Continuum International Publishing Group

The Tower Building   80 Maiden Lane
11 York Road   Suite 704, New York
London SE1 7NX   NY 10038

www.continuumbooks.com

British Library Cataloguing-in-Publication Data
A catalogue record for this book is available from the British Library.

ISBN: 978-0-8264-9647-8 (hardback)
       978-0-8264-9648-5 (paperback)

Library of Congress Cataloging-in-Publication Data
A catalog record for this book is available from the Library of Congress.

Typeset by Newgen Imaging Systems Pvt Ltd, Chennai, India
Printed and bound in Great Britain by MPG Books Ltd, Bodmin Cornwall

Contents

General Preface

Continuum Modern Theatre Guides

Volumes in the series Continuum Modern Theatre Guides offer concise and informed introductions to the key plays of modern times. Each book takes a close look at one particular play's dramaturgical qualities and then at its various theatrical manifestations. The books are carefully structured to offer a systematic study of the play in its biographical, historical, social and political context, followed by an in-depth study of the text and a chapter which outlines the work's production history, examining both the original productions of the play and subsequent major stage interpretations. Where relevant, screen adaptations will also be analyzed. There then follows a chapter dedicated to workshopping the play, based on suggested group exercises. Also included are a timeline and suggestions for further reading.

Each book covers:

- Background and context
- Analysis of the play
- Production history
- Workshopping exercises

The aim is to provide accessible introductions to modern plays for students in both Theatre/Performance Studies and English, as well as for informed general readers. The series includes up-to-date coverage of a broad range of key plays, with summaries of important

critical approaches and the intellectual debates that have illumi-
nated the meaning of the work and made a significant contribution
to our broader cultural life. They will enable readers to develop their
understanding of playwrights and theatre-makers, as well as inspir-
ing them to broaden their studies.

The Editors:
Steve Barfield, Janelle Reinelt,
Graham Saunders and Aleks Sierz

March 2008

Acknowledgements

I would like to begin by thanking the series editors and Continuum Press for affording me is opportunity. I must also express my extreme gratitude to Harry Elam, Jr for recommending for this project. I am extremely grateful to you all.

I would also like thank the August Wilson scholars, especially Sandra Shannon and Joan Herrington, who have served as my mentors. Your work has served as the foundation of scholarly endeavors.

I could not have completed this text without the support and guidance of my fences – my family, friends, and colleagues: Mark, Morgan and Madeline Furr, Gwendolyn Menson, Gail Furr and Gary Woolnough, Cheryl, Allen, Shaydra, and Shallene Joseph, Belinda S. Hodges, Pamela Segrest, Ruth Burkes, Father Colenzo Hubbard, Cassandra Turner, Verner Mitchell, Reginald Martin, Rebecca Argall, William Demastes, Reginald Brown, Verlinda Franklin, Carlotta Jones, Yvonne Draper, Susan Fitzgerald, Trellis Morgan, Lori Cohoon, Sarah Keith, Jervette Ward, Darrin Miller and Jonathan Wallace. I could not have completed any of this without you.

Janelle Reinhelt, Colleen Coalter and Anna Sandeman, thank you for all of your guidance and patience. I am indebted to you all.

All quotations from August Wilson's *Fences* copyright © 1986 by August Wilson appear with kind permission from Dutton Signet, a division of Penguin Group (USA) Inc.

LADRICA MENSON-FURR
Memphis, June 2008

1 Background and Context

This chapter will serve as a preliminary introduction to the study of August Wilson's *Fences*. It explains why the play is important, gives a sketch of Wilson's life, and discusses the social, economic and political background of the play.

Introduction

On 16 October 2005, New York City's historic Broadway theatre district added a new page to its annals and a new marquee to its locality. On this day, the former Virginia Theatre was renamed to honor the most celebrated African-American dramatist of the twentieth and early twenty-first century, August Wilson. The story of how this gentleman rose from obscurity to the Great White Way (Broadway's nickname) has been and will be told throughout dramatic and literary history, with particular emphasis on his entire dramatic canon, and especially on the drama *Fences*. Set in the Pittsburgh Hill District in 1957, *Fences* confirmed Wilson's presence in American mainstream theatre, and continued his journey towards Broadway immortality. Like the play's main character, Troy Maxson, Wilson's *Fences* has a wonderful history that simultaneously relays and reflects its significance within the records of American and world drama.

August Wilson's *Fences* was first produced in 1985 at the Yale Repertory Theatre under the directorial eye of Lloyd Richards. This production was the second of six works on which Wilson and Richards collaborated, and it contributed to the playwright being seen by some as 'America's greatest playwright' and the 'American

Shakespeare'. After the production of this play at Yale, Chicago's Goodman Theatre, the Seattle Repertory Theatre and in San Francisco, _Fences_ opened on Broadway at the 46th Street Theatre on 26 March 1987. _Fences_, however, is not only important because it secured Wilson's presence on Broadway, but also because it proved that another African-American playwright could meet the challenge and compose a traditional drama – one that revolved around the actions of one character – and write both himself and a new African-American protagonist, Troy Maxson, into the annals of American theatre alongside timeless characters such as Arthur Miller's Willie Loman and Lorraine Hansberry's Walter Lee Younger. _Fences_ also won the Pulitzer Prize for Drama (the second African-American authored drama to win this award), the New York Drama Critics' Circle Award, and four Tony awards (Best Actor: James Earl Jones; Best Actress: Mary Alice; Best Director: Lloyd Richards; and Best Play). Moreover, the drama demonstrated the universality of Wilson's African-American centered characters and cultures. _Fences_ is a play about father–son conflict, marital challenges, responsibility and forgiveness. It is a drama that, as its opening words state, exposes and simultaneously exorcises the sins of the father. Wilson writes, 'When the sins of our fathers visit us/We do not have to play host./We can banish them with forgiveness/As God, in His Largeness and Laws' (Wilson, 1985: 95). With these words he instructs his audiences to recognize their fathers' human frailties and seek a way to forgive and understand them.

Despite its numerous accolades, multi-million dollar earnings, and continued celebrated status, _Fences_ was Wilson's 'least favorite play' (Williams and Shannon, 2004: 194) and the work that he considered to be the 'odd man out' of his cycle of dramas. Thirteen days before _Fences's_ Broadway opening, Wilson explained to David Savran that _Fences_ was 'the odd one [play], more conventional in structure with its large character' (Savran, 1987: 30). He added that he wrote it in order to combat the criticism that _Fences's_ predecessor, _Ma Rainey's Black Bottom_, had an 'oddly structured' plot. Similarly,

Wilson told Dennis Watlington that *Fences* was not the type of play that he 'wanted to write,' but after telling people that he could compose a more conventional play, he wrote *Fences* in order to prove to himself that he could (Watlington, 1989: 88). In 1993, 6 years after its successful Broadway run, Wilson reassessed *Fences* as the odd man out and asserted that:

> If you pull *Fences* out, a more natural progression of my work would have been from *Ma Rainey* to *Joe Turner* to *The Piano Lesson*. And yet *Fences* can also be the fulcrum, the centerpiece, the thing upon which everything turns. In other words, if you're fashioning a chain or something, I'm not sure that *Fences* should necessarily be the odd man out. Maybe we need another similar kind of play that would balance it or complement it . . .. My challenge now would be to write another one, to find a character that is as representative of black America in the eighties as Troy was in the fifties. (Richard Pettengill, 1993: 167)

Thus, *Fences* began as a challenge, yet became the centerpiece of the ten-play cycle that he would conclude with *Radio Golf.*

About the play's author

In artistic and literary eyes, the month of April is associated with rebirth, regeneration, the color green, the warmth of the sun, the melting of the snow and the promise of spring. Frederick August Kittel was born in the spring of 1945, on 27 April in the ethnically diverse Hill District of Pittsburgh, Pennsylvania. The Hill District of 1945 reflected the after effects of the Great Migration of African Americans from the South to North and the immigration of German, Italian and Irish people into the United States. The first ethnic group to settle in the Hill District was comprised of Jewish emigrants, between 1870 and 1890, 'followed by Italians, Greeks, Syrians, and Poles' (Pittsburgh Neighborhood Alliance, 1977: 2). African Americans began to settle in this area as early as the 1880s and on through the 1960s in search of the better jobs, educational opportunities for their children, and to escape the increasing disenfranchisement and segregation legislation (known as Jim Crow Laws) that dominated much of the American South from the 1890s until the Civil Rights Movement began in the 1950s. Kittel's parents, Daisy Wilson Kittel, an African-American domestic worker, and Frederick Kittel, a German baker, raised him and his five siblings in the Hill District and in the Pittsburgh suburb of Hazelwood. Later, Daisy Wilson and her children returned to the Hill District, and Frederick August Kittel adopted his mother's maiden name and became known as August Wilson.

While little is known about Wilson's father, most biographers have noted his red hair and his frequent absences from the Kittel household. While Wilson explored father–son conflicts in his works, particularly in *Fences* and *Jitney*, his dramas do not explicitly explore the issue of the missing German father. Film and stage actor and director Charles Dutton, speaking at the 2005 Situating August Wilson in the Canon and in the Curriculum Symposium (hosted by Dr Sandra Shannon and Howard University), noted that this aspect of Wilson's life has not been explored. I assume that Dutton means that Wilson, at least dramatically, had not explored the realities of interracial families (Menson-Furr, 2005: conference notes). Hence, Wilson's dramatic world is not a complete representation of his life (nor should it be). More, however, is known about Wilson's stepfather, David Bedford, who became one of many surrogate fathers who helped to shape the young Frederick Kittel's masculine self. Wilson's mother, Daisy Wilson Kittel Bedford, also remains largely an anonymous figure in Wilson's biographies, but her presence and her teachings loom large in Kittel's/Wilson's evolution from man-child to man.

August Wilson completed his education within the school of urban, American realism. In 1959, he left Central Catholic High School, where he was the only black student, because of numerous threats and abuse. One year later, the 15-year-old Wilson 'resigned' from the Pittsburgh educational system after being accused of plagiarizing a 20-page essay on Napoleon. Wilson then turned to Pittsburgh's Carnegie Library, particularly its Negro Section, where he read the works of Ralph Ellison, Langston Hughes and Richard Wright (Wolfe, 1999: 2). He also immersed himself in the pool halls, restaurants, and streets of the Hill District, and, as some Wilson-scholars state, earned his high school and college credentials within their walls. Wilson's Hill District experiences, lessons and teachers provided him with models for many of the characters, stories and subjects that dominate his dramatic works.

Between 1962 and 1963, Wilson enlisted and served in the United States Army. Following his discharge, he worked various odd jobs including stints as a porter, a short-order cook, a gardener and dishwasher. He also began writing poetry, inspired by Dylan Thomas, his favorite poet.

In 1965, at the age of 20, August Wilson began writing for the stage. In the same year, Frederick Kittel died, and his son Frederick August Kittel changed his name to August Wilson. He moved into a rooming house on Pittsburgh's Bedford Avenue, and began his writing career as poet with the purchase of his first type-writer (for 20 dollars). Wilson also discovered the blues and Bessie Smith's 'Nobody Can Bake a Sweet Jelly Roll Like Mine' after pur-chasing a record player and a stack of blues records. He fondly relays this story and the affects of the blues on both him his work:

In 1965, as a twenty-year-old poet living in a rooming house in Pittsburgh, I discovered Bessie Smith and the blues. It was a watershed event in my life. It gave me a history. It provided me with a cultural response to the world as well as the knowledge that the text and content of my life were worthy of the highest celebration and occasion of art. It also gave me a framework and an aesthetic for exploring the tradition from which it grew. I set out on a continual search for ways to give expression to the spiritual impulse of the African-American culture which had nurtured and sanctioned my life and ultimately provided it with its meaning. I was, as are all artists, searching for a way to define myself in relation to the world I lived in. The blues gave me a firm and secure ground. It became, and remains, the wellspring of my art. (Wilson, 1990 in *Romare Bearden: His Life and Art*: 8 'Foreword')

The musical genre of the blues is integral to understanding Wilson's dramatic perspective and his dramatic/cultural philosophy. The blues became one of Wilson's first dramatic influences and the literal soundtrack of his planned and completed ten-play cycle.

In 1968, Wilson and his friend Rob Penny founded the Black Horizons Theater company. The Black Horizons Theater emerged in the midst of the Black Arts/Black Aesthetic movement which would yield Wilson his second dramatic influence – the work of Amiri Baraka (Leroi Jones). 'Baraka's influence,' according to Wilson, 'has less to do with the way that he writes and more to do with the ideas that he espoused in the '60s as a black nationalist – ideas that I found value in then and still find value in' (Shannon, 1993: 554).

Wilson's playwrighting career began in earnest in 1973, when he wrote his first play, *Recycle*, and in 1976 his play, *The Homecoming*, was directed by Vernell Little for the Kuntu Repertory Theatre. Also in this year, Wilson watched *Sizwe Bansi Is Dead*, the first professionally staged play he had seen, and encountered another influence on his work, South-African dramatist Athol Fugard. He composed a musical satire, 'Black Bart and the Sacred Hills', in 1977 and moved to St Paul, Minnesota a year later where he wrote children's plays for the Minnesota Science Museum. During this time Wilson also wrote the play *Jitney* (1979), the only one of his dramas written during the decade of its setting. While Wilson's dramatic cycle was greatly influenced by the blues and the nationalistic perspectives of Amiri Baraka and Athol Fugard, his strongest visual inspiration was found within the works of visual artist Romare Bearden, whom he considered a mentor. The play *Joe Turner's Come and Gone* and the characters Seth and Bertha Holly were inspired by Bearden's collages 'Mill Hand's Lunch Bucket' and 'Mr Seth and Miss Bertha', and the title of *The Piano Lesson* came from Bearden's collage of the same name. Wilson first encountered Bearden's work in *The Prevalence of Ritual*, a printed collection of his art works, placed on a table at the home of his friend, Claude Purdy:

> In 1977 . . . I discovered the art of Romare Bearden. My friend . . . had purchased a copy of *The Prevalence of Ritual*, and one night, in the Fall of 1977, after dinner and much talk, he laid it open on the table before me. 'Look at this', he said. 'Look at this'. I looked. What for me had been so difficult, Bearden made seem so simple, so easy. What I saw was black life presented on its own terms, on a grand and epic scale, with all its richness and fullness, in a language that was vibrant and which, made attendant to everyday life, ennobled it, affirmed its value, and exalted its presence. . . . In Bearden I found my artistic mentor and sought, and still aspire, to make my plays the equal of his canvases . . . (Wilson, 1990: 8–9)

August Wilson's playwriting talents continued to be honed during the 1980s, when he was awarded a Fellowship at the Minneapolis Playwrights Center (1980) and witnessed *Jitney's* staging in Pittsburgh at the Allegheny Repertory Theatre. Wilson's play *Ma Rainey's Black Bottom* was accepted by the National Playwrights Conference at the O'Neill Theater Center in Connecticut in 1982. This play became Wilson's first commercially successful drama and began his six-play collaboration with former O'Neill Center chief and Dean of the Yale School of Drama, Lloyd Richards.

From 1984 to 2005, August Wilson's dramas and name rose from obscurity to critical acclaim. After the successful Yale Repertory Theatre, regional theatre and Broadway runs of _Ma Rainey's Black Bottom_, Wilson composed the dramas _Fences_, _Joe Turner's Come and Gone_, _The Piano Lesson_, _Two Trains Running_, _Seven Guitars_, _Jitney_ (revised), _King Hedley II_, _Gem of the Ocean_ and lastly _Radio Golf_.

August Wilson was diagnosed with liver cancer on 16 June 2005. He died at the Swedish Medical Center in Seattle, Washington, on 2 October 2005. Wilson's life reads like one of his great stage dramas and reflects the success of the American dream – the American dramatic dream – of an African-American male born in 1945. In the autumn of his life, Wilson was able to witness the completion of his cycle of plays – his plan and his goal. He completed his historic fence of twentieth-century African-American dramatic history and left the gate open for all of us to enter.

The social, economic and political context

Wilson offers an historical and political contextualization for _Fences_ in the section 'The Play' in the published text: 'By 1957, the hard-won victories of the European immigrants had solidified the industrial might of America. War had been confronted and won with new energies that used loyalty and patriotism as its fuel. Life was rich, full, and flourishing' (103). By 1957, America had fought and won two wars – World War I and World War II – and had continued to construct itself into a Western 'super power'. The country's president, Dwight D. Eisenhower, began radical changes within the social infrastructure at home, especially as the walls of southern segregatory laws began to crumble following the United States Supreme Court's historic 1954 ruling in the Brown vs. the Topeka Board of Education case, in which they reversed the 'separate but equal' legislation that had pervaded the South. President Eisenhower declared that 'there must be no second class citizens in this country' (www.whitehouse.gov). He ordered the complete desegregation of the American Armed Forces and sent Federal Troops to Little Rock, Arkansas, to make certain that the state complied with Federal Law and to protect the students who would be christened 'The Little Rock Nine' and become the first black students to enroll at Little Rock's Central High School (www.whitehouse.gov). Hence, Wilson situates *Fences* among the winds of change that propel Troy Maxson, a native southerner, to ask Mr Rand, his white employer, the simple questions, 'Why? Why you got the white mens driving and the colored lifting?' (106). After following Rand's instructions to 'take it to the union' (106), Troy migrates from the back of the truck as a garbage can lifter, to the front of the truck as a driver.

For African Americans, the 1950s were still wrought with continued discrimination, disenfranchisement and political and economic strife. African-American men had now served in two world wars, but following both battles they returned to a country that continued to judge them by the color of their skin. The second wave of the Great Migration began during this time as African Americans began to migrate both to the West and the North. More and more African Americans began to fight for economic and political rights by organizing, boycotting businesses that refused to serve them, and staging protest marches and sit-ins. However, it must be noted that African Americans did not begin these revolutionary activities in the 1950s. Historians have documented that during the Transatlantic slave trade and period of American Slavery (1619–1865), African Americans organized, battled their oppressors, and fought – physically and legally – for the rights to vote, educate their children, purchase their family members and own land. Thus, by the 1950s, African Americans had inherited a long legacy of activism that began in the twentieth century with African-American leaders (often called 'race men' and 'race women') such as W. E. B. Du Bois, Booker T. Washington, James Weldon Johnson, Ida B. Wells-Barnett and Mary McLeod Bethune, who were fighting for equality and basic human rights in both the North and the South.

The decade of the 1950s was also the grandchild of the Harlem Renaissance and its 'New Negro', the new generation of African-American artists and intellectuals emerging in the 1920s (Alain Locke, 1925: 960–70). The Harlem Renaissance was an artistic and political movement that celebrated African-American art, music, dance and literature alongside strategies for social and political uplift. The movement aimed to demonstrate, in the words of Harlem Renaissance poet Langston Hughes, that African Americans did 'too, sing America' (Hughes, 1925, 1959: 1295).

Fences is set two years before the debut of Lorraine Hansberry's groundbreaking _A Raisin in the Sun_ on Broadway (1959) and three years prior to the beginning of the American Black Arts Movement (1960s). Wilson reminds his audience, 'the hot winds of change that would make the sixties a turbulent, racing, dangerous, and provocative decade had not yet begun to blow full' (104). Troy Maxson's demand for equality and the play's powerful illustration of African-American manhood is only a minute foreshadowing of the eruptions that occurred during the decade of the 1960s. Indicative of the turbulence and violence, President John F. Kennedy (1963) and African-American leaders Malcolm X (1964) and Martin Luther King, Jr (1968) were assassinated.

Wilson begins _Fences_ at the turn of the twentieth century and traces the evolution of Pittsburgh's population from European immigrants to the masses of African Americans who would find their way from the American South to the American North as they participated in what is now known as The Great Migration. The (first) Great Migration took place between 1916 and 1930. Angry, frightened, disenfranchised, and disappointed by the false promises of emancipation and the continued antagonism of segregation, the Ku Klux Klan and Jim Crow, African Americans moved away from the South in search of a better life, one free of the burden of southern racial discrimination. Approximately 1.5 million African Americans moved from the southern states of Tennessee, Alabama, Georgia, Mississippi and Louisiana to the nearest northern states, such as Ohio and Illinois, and then further northward into Pennsylvania, Michigan and New York. These migrants walked, drove and rode the northern bound trains in search of the promises of the North, yet many found the North to be a challenging terrain to traverse – racially, economically and environmentally. As Wilson explained:

> The city rejected them, and they fled and settled along the riverbanks and under bridges in shallow, ramshackle houses made of sticks and tar-paper. They collected rags and wood. They sold the use of their muscles and their bodies. They cleaned houses and washed clothes, they shined shoes, and in quiet desperation and vengeful pride, they stole and lived in pursuit of their own dream: That they could breathe free, finally, and stand to meet life with the force of dignity and whatever eloquence the heart could call upon. (103)

This group of Pittsburgh residents not only became the focus of *Fences*, but also of eight additional Wilson plays, that would fittingly comprise what has been identified as the 'Pittsburgh Cycle' (*Gem of the Ocean, Joe Turner's Come and Gone, The Piano Lesson, Seven Guitars, Two Trains Running, Jitney, King Hedley II, and Radio Golf*). *Fences* is the first commercially produced Wilson drama to introduce the character and strengths of this group of individuals that survived life in a country that used their bodies, and then refused to embrace them as its own.

Wilson's twentieth-century cycle

Each play of August Wilson's twentieth-century cycle presents an episode from each decade of the African-American experience between the years 1900 and 2000 (specifically 1904–1995). An interdisciplinary amalgam of African-American history, sociology, musicology and literature, each play within the cycle offers its audiences the opportunity to begin to understand the emotional, psychological and physical effects that African Americans harbor, consciously and unconsciously, from both the African continent and the American homeland. Wilson's cycle also serves as a conduit to the African continent, by way of the American South, the place that Wilson viewed as the African-American's first point of origin. The cycle's intent is to celebrate the uniqueness of African-American culture and its people, its survivors, and specifically to recognize that African Americans are humans who possess the capacity to harm, be harmed, hurt and heal just as all other beings. Interestingly, Wilson began composing his cycle of plays by way of 'coincidence'. He explained to Sandra Shannon that he 'didn't start out with a grand idea' to compose a cycle. Instead, he tells Shannon, 'I wrote a play called *Jitney!* set in '71, and a play called *Fullerton Street* that I set in '41. Then I wrote *Ma Rainey's Black Bottom*, which I set in '27, and it was after I did that I said, "I've written three plays in three different decades, so why don't I just continue to do that?"' (Shannon, 1991: 120). Thus, as Wilson composed dramas that reached back into the history of his people, he identified a course that had already been chartered for him by the experiences of African Americans through their histories. He became the medium for these voices and their stories.

Wilson's twentieth-century cycle, although including a play reflecting each decade in the twentieth century, was not written in chronological order. Thus, the following discussion of the plays will trace the cycle as it was composed and, with the exception of *Jitney*, produced.

Ma Rainey's Black Bottom (1984), set in 1927, was Wilson's first commercially successful drama and examined the blues and the blues musicians who comprised the band of the famous blues songstress Gertrude 'Ma' Rainey. This drama illustrates Wilson's signature ensemble play style enhanced with major Wilsonian monologues that make his characters and their words into distinctive voices. Filled with music, history and important reminders about the exploitation of blues performers, *Ma Rainey's Black Bottom* both resurrects the 'sass' and business acumen possessed by the historical Madame Rainey, and enables Wilson's blues men to articulate their blues to a wide theatre audience. Under the direction of Lloyd Richards, *Ma Rainey's Black Bottom* opened on Broadway at the Cort Theatre on 11 October 1984. The play was revived in 2003 at the Royale Theatre, running from 22 January to 6 April 2003, starring Whoopi Goldberg as Gertrude 'Ma Rainey' and Charles Dutton reviving his original performance as Levee.

Joe Turner's Come and Gone (1988), set in 1914, followed the same regional theatre path as *Fences,* and was written and workshopped while *Fences* was being performed on Broadway. This drama, the second play in the cycle from the standpoint of chronology, takes its audiences back in time to the first wave of the Great Migration to follow the trails of the numerous southerners migrating away from the Jim Crow South towards the promises of the great, industrial northern cities. *Joe Turner's Come and Gone* blends both the African and African-American pasts, and the southern and northern migrants' quests for an identity into a complex drama that requires its audiences to understand the long-term repercussions of slavery, the Reconstruction period and the Great Migration.

In several interviews Wilson identified *Joe Turner's Come and Gone* as his favorite play, and the play that should have logically followed *Ma Rainey's Black Bottom*. Returning to the ensemble cast, this drama combines African-American folklore, a West African ring shout dance called the Juba, and a very complex clash of African spirituality, Christianity and 'conjuring'. *Joe Turner's Come and Gone* illustrated Wilson's determination to reclaim the Africanness of the African-American past, and to demonstrate the effects of nineteenth-century slavery and twentieth-century slavery/indentured servitude on many African-American men.

The Piano Lesson (1990), inspired by the collage of the same name created by Romare Bearden, continues Wilson's discussions of legacies, family and the importance of acknowledging and embracing the past in order to exist in the present and future. While *Fences* centers on a father–son conflict, *The Piano Lesson* examines a brother–sister conflict and the question of 'How does one build upon his/her legacy?' At the center of this drama is, as its title discloses, a piano that holds separate, but communal, meanings for the Charles family. Thus far, *The Piano Lesson* is the only play in the cycle that has been adapted for film or television. Wilson composed the Hallmark Hall of Fame's teleplay for the adaptation, and the production included most of the original Broadway cast.

Two Trains Running (1992), set in 1968, following the assassinations of Dr Martin Luther King, Jr and Malcolm X, 'picks up the ball' of Wilson's works and continues to ask the question of what do we do with our legacies. At this point in Wilson's dramatic history, blacks are continuing to fight for their Civil Rights, but they have in many instances forgotten who they are and where they come from. With the leaders towards progress gone, the African-American struggle may regress if its members don't, in the words of the mystical Aunt Ester, 'You got to go back and pick up the ball' (Wilson, 1993: 109), reclaiming their histories, their identities and themselves. *Two Trains Running*, like each of Wilson's early works, continues the blues theme, especially in its title, which refers to the physical trains moving back and forth between the North and South weekly, while also evoking the train's presence that is imperative to blues music.

The play *Seven Guitars* (1996) follows some of the techniques of Argentinean writer Jorge Luis Borges. According to Joan Herrington, 'Borges and Wilson are more concerned with how things happen than with what actually happens. Wilson was specifically influenced by Borges's technique of revealing the ending of his stories in the first lines, which forces the reader to focus on the process and not the outcome' (Herrington, 1998: 4). As a result of this influence, in *Seven Guitars* the end of the play is the play's beginning, and the plot unfolds through flashbacks to the life and the events preceding the death of the blues musician Floyd 'School Boy' Barton. Wilson says that he was 'fascinated with the way Borges . . . tells a story . . . He tells you exactly what is going to happen, even though the outcome may seem improbable . . . See, if you write a play like that, the audience will be just intrigued with trying to . . . So then you become intrigued just sitting there trying to figure it out' (Shannon, 1993: 554–55).

Jitney, set in 1971, was the first of Wilson's twentieth-century cycle plays and the only drama that was written during the decade in which it was set. Written in 1979, *Jitney* was rejected twice by the Eugene O'Neill Center before Wilson wrote *Ma Rainey's Black and Bottom* and it was the seventh play to be staged. *Jitney* revisits the father–son conflict theme that would be introduced in *Fences* and illuminates the entrepreneurial spirit possessed by many of Wilson's disenfranchised warrior characters. Centered upon a Jitney cab operation, owned and managed by Becker and staffed by several independent contractors, *Jitney* asks and answers Marvin Gaye's musical question of the 1970s, 'What's Goin' On?' and continues *Two Trains Running*'s advice to 'pick up the ball' (Wilson, 1993: 109) despite your past. *Jitney*, like most of Wilson's dramas, concludes with death, but from each death the sprit of hope emerges for both the audience and at least one character on the stage.

Jitney was also the only Wilson drama that was not produced on Broadway. Instead, after being produced at numerous regional theatres, *Jitney* began its New York run Off-Broadway at the Second Stage Theatre, opening on 25 April 2000 and then migrated to Off-Broadway's larger Union Square Theatre where it re-opened on 19 September 2000. *Jitney* was directed by Marion McClinton (who later directed the television version of *The Piano Lesson*).

King Hedley II (1998), set in 1985, is arguably the sequel to Wilson's *Seven Guitars* and his second attempt to compose a drama that centered on one character. Directed by Marion McClinton, King Hedley II follows the life and frustrations of Ruby's son and Hedley's namesake, King Hedley II, as he attempts to secure the American Dream in 1985. Surviving in the midst of rising black-on-black crime, especially between young black men, and a legacy of economic disenfranchisement and incarceration, King finds himself at odds with his wife, mother, friends, neighbors and the world at large. Like all of Wilson's plays, King Hedley II is a tragedy that ends with a death, King's death, but also suggests that the spilled blood or lost life might help to create a different legacy. King Hedley II opened at Broadway's Virginia Theatre on 1 May 2001.

Gem of the Ocean (2003), set in 1904, is the drama that chronologically begins Wilson's twentieth-century cycle. Formally introducing the character of Aunt Ester who is first introduced in *Two Trains Running* and *King Hedley II*, the drama illustrates Wilson's ability to connect the African past with the African American presence in America and the twentieth century. In this drama, 287 year old Aunt Ester helps the troubled Citizen Barlow reconnect to his history as an African in America so that he may find his identity and life's purpose. Directed by Kenny Leon, the drama opened at Broadway's Walter Kerr Theatre on December 6, 2004, but closed on February 6, 2005 after 15 preview performances and 72 regular performances (Simonson, 2005: www.playbill.com 06 February 2005).

Radio Golf (2007) is the right-side 'bookend' of August Wilson's American cycle dramas. This play returns to Aunt Ester's 1839 Wylie Avenue residence, now a dilapidated edifice, and, fittingly, reflects on the state of African-American culture and Aunt Ester's descendants at the cusp of the twenty-first century. Continuing Wilson's focus on African-American cultural legacies, *Radio Golf's* main character, Harmon Wilkes, has benefited from the progress that Wilson's characters have made since the 1904 set *Gem of the Ocean*, but he has become disconnected from his past, his ancestors and the very spirit of Aunt Ester. Instead of ending in tragedy, this drama ends with a celebration as Harmon Wilkes, Aunt Ester's descendant, 'picks up the paintbrush' and, instead of demolishing her home, joins the movement to preserve it and his cultural legacy.

Radio Golf opened on 8 May 2007 at Broadway's Cort Theatre. Directed by Kenny Leon, *Radio Golf* won the New York Drama Critics' Circle award for Best American Play. It received four TONY award nominations, and nominations from the Drama Desk, Drama League and Outer Critics Circle.

2 Analysis and Commentary

This chapter is a study of *Fences* both as a dramatic text and as a performed play that has excited comment and provoked analysis. Although plot summaries are often seen as old-fashioned, they are useful in sketching out the action of the play before undertaking a broader analysis of its characters, influences, images, themes and key scenes.

Plot summary

Fences begins in 1957, and chronicles the last 8 years in the life of its protagonist, Troy Maxson, and the effects of his decisions and actions upon his family. Maxson is one of the many southern migrants who struggled to forge a place for himself in the North, specifically in the Pittsburgh Hill District. In the play's exposition we learn that, at the age of 14, Troy Maxson walked 200 miles to Mobile, Alabama, and joined a group of southern migrants heading North. Once he reached the North, Troy, like many African-American transplants, found few if any of the promises that the destination promised. He was forced to steal in order to eat, and then after meeting the woman who would become his first wife and fathering a son, Lyons, he was forced to steal to feed three mouths. While stealing to feed his family, Troy commits murder and is sentenced to 15 years in the state penitentiary. In the penitentiary Troy discovers the sport that he would use to explain his life, baseball, and after his release, he plays for a time in the American Negro Baseball League. During his incarceration, his first wife moved on without him; however, his luck improved when he met the woman who would become his second wife, Rose. Together, they have created a second opportunity for Troy to live a semblance of the American dream – a family, a home and a job – complete with a second son, Cory.

Act One, Scene One

The action of the play begins on a Friday in 1957. It is pay day for Troy Maxson and his long-time friend, Jim Bono. During this weekly ritual of celebrating the 'eagle's flying' (a colloquial phrase that means pay day), Troy and Bono share a pint of whiskey and Troy, through 'tall talk', slips into and out of the role of storyteller as he verbally vacillates between his present actions and his past. Wilson's stage directions aptly explain the crux of this scene which is dominated largely by Troy's perspectives on work, life, death and love: '*TROY is fifty-three years old, a large man with thick, heavy hands: it is this largeness that strives to fill out and make an accommodation with. Together with his blackness, his largeness informs his sensibilities and the choices he has made in his life*' (105).

This scene introduces Bono (Troy's friend of three decades), Rose (Troy's devoted wife), Lyons (Troy's son from his first marriage) and Troy's voice as a character who attempts to control everyone's perceptions. Troy has an audience, and he offers them an excellent one-man show in which he depicts an activist-trash collector, a warrior who was bold enough to fight with death and win, a human who met the devil and lived to tell about it, and an intellectual who can analyze and question the concept of time as it applies to and controls a man's desires.

In this scene, Troy illustrates his opinionated contrariness as he shuns his second son's, Cory's, possibilities for an athletic scholarship, dismisses the fact that age prevented him from playing baseball professionally, and lastly, criticizes Lyons's desire to live as a focused musician who thinks it is okay to borrow money from his father and live off of his woman. Beyond Troy's storytelling, this scene reaches its pinnacle during the drama's first conflict – a verbal between Troy and Lyons.

Lyons has come to borrow money from his father, but before he can secure the loan he has to listen to Troy's evaluation of his character. Lyons's response to his father foreshadows the image of Troy Maxson that will evolve in the play's remaining scenes. Lyons sees nothing wrong with his decisions, but Troy thinks that scolding his adult son will encourage him to reform. Lyons, however, reminds Troy that he is too old to change, and that Troy was absent during his youth. Hence, Troy's opinion is invalid. Troy offers Lyons sound advice, but Lyons's response reminds Troy and everyone witnessing this exchange that, as Lyons states, 'You and me is two different people, Pop,' and that Troy's proscriptions about life and work are a 'day late and dollar short' (119). Troy loses this father–son conflict, but he brushes away this loss and returns to his 'manly banter'.

Act One, Scene Two

This scene begins the next morning, Saturday, with Rose in the yard hanging laundry on the clothesline and singing an African-American spiritual that contains the drama's titular metaphor: 'Jesus, be a fence all around me everyday . . .' (122). Troy enters the scene from the house in a contentious mood. Rose thinks he is concerned about his talk with Mr Rand, his supervisor, but Troy denies this concern. Gabriel, Troy's brother and one of Wilson's most fascinating spectacle characters, enters the drama in this scene and ushers in a compelling sub-plot. (Wilson's spectacle characters are characters who appear to sit on the periphery of sanity, but who, along with his plot's main protagonist, often motivate the plot's action and offer the drama's most insightful and compelling perspectives.) Gabriel, a disabled war veteran, believes that he has died, gone to heaven and has been reincarnated as the Archangel Gabriel. He enters the drama and informs Troy that St Peter has his name (and Rose's) written in his book. When Rose instructs him to go inside the house so that she may prepare a proper meal for him, he refuses because he has to keep peddling his wares so that he can save up enough money to purchase a new horn 'so St Peter can hear me when it's time to open the gates' (127). Gabriel exits this scene singing a spiritual with the refrain, 'Better get ready for the judgment . . . My God is coming down' (127).

After Gabriel's departure, Rose and Troy discuss Gabriel's physical and mental state. Rose tells Troy that Gabriel would be better cared for in a hospital, but Troy defends his brother's right to independence, especially since he was wounded while serving in his country's armed forces. Troy's contentious mood returns because he is embarrassed and angered as the only reason he has a home is because he benefited from his brother's veteran's benefits. He would not have anything if it were not for Gabriel's war induced madness. This scene concludes with a frustrated Troy headed for Taylor's Bar to listen to a baseball game.

Act One, Scene Three

This scene takes place 4 hours later, on the same Saturday. Rose is in the yard removing clothing from the clothesline when Cory returns from football practice. She informs him that Troy is upset with him for not completing his morning chores, and suggests that he quickly change his clothing, eat and get to work before his father returns from Taylor's. After Cory enters the house, Troy enters the yard. He is in a jovial mood, and affectionately chases Rose around. He then summons Cory to begin his Saturday chore: constructing the fence. Father and son are now alone in the yard, but what begins as a poignant father–son moment in which Troy advises Cory about good financial practices and even makes a deal with him to purchase a television set, quickly becomes a father–son conflict. Troy begins scolding Cory for neglecting his chores in favor of football. He does not support Cory's reverence for football because he fears that

Cory will be exploited by the white-controlled sports industry. Also, because of his missed opportunity to play in the integrated professional baseball league, he does not want Cory to buy into the pipe dream that professional sports often offers to black men. Instead, Troy wants Cory to continue to excel in school, retain his job at the local A&P, and after graduation find a solid career with A&P or in a trade.

Troy's tirade continues after Cory, innocently, asks him, 'How come you ain't never liked me?' (135). Instead of eliciting the expected sympathetic response, Troy morphs into a cruel and seemingly unloving parent who instead of making his son feel loved, uses this question to teach him a crude, but valid, lesson about responsibility and fairness. Troy's advice is sound, but his delivery is venomous and leaves Cory feeling rejected.

Rose overhears this exchange and tries to explain to Troy that Cory wants to know that Troy is proud of him. Troy, as he did with Lyons, offers sound but cruelly delivered wisdom when he says that he wants Cory to be better than he is, both professionally and humanely. Instead of apologizing to Rose or Cory for his behavior, this scene concludes with Troy's almost hopeless recapitulation of his daily woes.

Act One, Scene Four

Two weeks have passed and it is Friday, pay day, for Troy and Bono. Together the two enter the yard with their pay, but Troy has extra compensation, for he is now a rubbish truck driver. When the drama began, Troy asked Mr Rand why the whites were drivers and the blacks were the lifters. Mr Rand told him to take it up with union; Troy did, and the union made Troy a first in Hill District African-American history – the first black driver. Troy calls Rose to the yard to share the good news, Lyons arrives shortly thereafter to repay his father and invites him to hear him perform, and Gabe enters bequeathing Rose a flower. Thus, Troy's audience is assembled once again. Along with the story of his recent success, Troy begins narrating another story, but this is a painful one.

Troy relays the story of his youth as a sharecropper's son. Proudly he asserts that his father did not leave his family – eleven children – but he admits that his father was bitter and mean. He applauds his father's sense of responsibility, and is proud that he learned this lesson from him and carried it with him even after he was 'banished' from home. For the first time in the drama, Troy's character becomes sympathetic as he unfolds how, at the age of 14, he became a man. His passage into manhood was a violent beating at his father's hands, after he attempted to hit his father. Troy says that after he regained consciousness, he could not return home and for this reason, in 1918, he set out for Mobile (Alabama) and then began his journey Northward. Rose and Gabe are inside of the house, but Bono and Lyons hear this tale. Troy continues his story (Rose has now re-joined his audience) and tells the assemblage how he ended up in Pittsburgh, the penitentiary, and finally with Rose.

This scene, probably the drama's longest, continues after Bono and Lyons exit the yard, and Cory enters, angrily, from football practice. Troy, after learning that Cory has lied to him about quitting the football team and returning to his job at the A&P, obstructs Cory's scholarship opportunity. Cory accuses Troy of jealousy and fear that he will be better than he is. Troy tells Cory to 'come here' (153), but Rose intervenes, and Troy issues Cory a verbal warning that he has just made his first strike. He challenged and criticized his father – Troy Maxson, the boss – so he had better be careful.

Fences director, Lloyd Richards, explains that *Fences* is a play about the lessons that Troy Maxson learns from his bitter, 'sharecropper father': 'violence . . . the value of work . . . and responsibility' (Richards, 1985: Introduction). Act One, Scenes Three and Four, illustrate this theme and set the stage for the forthcoming 'battle royal' between Troy and Cory.

Act Two, Scene One

This act begins on a Saturday, 2 weeks have passed. Rose and Cory are in the yard discussing Cory's refusal to follow his father's instructions that he quit the football team. Always the referee between Troy and Cory, Rose offers to speak to Troy. Troy and Bono enter the yard. They have just returned from paying Gabriel's bail bond after he had been arrested and charged with 'disturbing the peace' (155). The two immediately resume construction on the Maxsons' fence. Bono uses this opportunity to discuss Troy's relationship with Alberta, his mistress. He explains to Troy that after he selected Rose to be his wife, he knew that Troy was good model of manhood. Hence, he decided that '[he] was gonna follow this nigger . . . he might take me somewhere' (158). He advises Troy to be careful not to ruin his marriage, and reminds him that 'Rose a good woman' (158). Subtly, Bono also asks Troy to avoid shattering the heroic image that he has of him. Bono exits and Rose enters the yard so that she and Troy may continue their discussion about Gabriel. Troy badly handles the segue from this discussion into an opportunity to tell her about his affair with Alberta and impending fatherhood.

This scene, which began with Troy's frustration with the law, now explodes with Rose's anger and resentment as she responds to Troy's declaration that he is not willing to give up Alberta. A major point of conflict, this scene places Rose against Troy in a verbal war, spoken in two languages: Rose's language is about love and family; Troy's language is riddled with baseball metaphors. This scene concludes with a second impending battle between Troy and Cory. Troy grabs Rose's arm and after hearing her cries, Cory exits from the house, grabs his father from behind, and punches him in the chest ('Stage Directions', in Wilson, 1985: 166). Troy rises to spar with his son but Rose, again the referee, holds him back as he informs Cory that he now has two strikes against him.

Act Two, Scene Two

This scene is set 6 months later, on the day that Alberta gives birth to Raynell. Troy is on his way to visit Alberta when Rose stops him to ask if he plans to come home from work on the next day, pay day Friday. Troy responds that he always comes home and that he always brings his pay to Rose, but he needs his space. Rose then accuses Troy of signing a form that would allow Gabriel to be committed to the mental hospital, a deal which would provide Troy with half of Gabe's monthly assistance check. Although Troy did sign the form, he contradicts himself as he, first, denies this act then states that he cannot read; therefore, he did not know what he signed. Rose dismisses his claim and accuses him of harming Gabe in the same way that he has hurt Cory; he signed for one but refused to sign for the other. In the midst of this battle, they are interrupted by the telephone. Rose answers the call and returns to the yard to tell Troy that the hospital phoned to say that Alberta has died, but the baby is fine. After Rose re-enters the house, Troy's anger rises and he informs Death that he is going to build a fence around his home, and commands Death to remain outside of the fence until he (Death) is ready to do battle with him.

Act Two, Scene Three

This is *Fences's* most succinct scene, but it is also one of the most powerful scenes in all of Wilson's dramas. If this scene had a title it would be 'Rose's Stance', for with few words and actions Rose dominates this scene and places Troy in a position of powerlessness. Three days after his daughter's birth, Troy brings the infant to the Maxson home and asks Rose to 'help me care for her' (173). Rose responds, 'you can't visit the sins of the father upon the child . . .' and her final pronouncement, 'the child got a mother. But you a womanless man' (173), inverts *Fences's* existing power structure. Rose's simultaneous adoption of Raynell and 'divorce' from Troy is powerful illustration of her character's strength, a strength that was up to this point in the drama overshadowed by Troy. Rose wins this battle, but Troy's war continues.

Act Two, Scene Four

Two months have passed. Cory, now a high-school graduate, is searching for a job, Rose is mothering the infant Raynell and Troy spends his Friday evenings alone, for Bono has found a new Friday night activity. This scene may be considered both *Fences's* denouement and central rising action, because Troy and Cory have their final standoff. In this scene, Rose, with Raynell in tow, leaves home to drop off a cake at the church and Troy and Cory are left alone. This time no referee will stop the fight.

Troy is sitting on the steps, drinking and singing his theme song 'Old Blue' when Cory attempts to 'walk over' him (178) to get into the house. Troy finds Cory's act to be disrespectful, and the two begin a verbal war that turns physical. This time Troy is the victor. While the first battles between the two were primarily verbal, this last battle involves a weapon – Troy's bat – and results in banishment. Troy tells Cory it is time for him to leave the home, to which Cory responds with a litany of Troy's hypocrisies. Troy grows angrier, and the battle turns physical. Troy shoves Cory. Cory takes up the bat, then swings at his father but misses. Troy grabs the bat and raises it to swing at his son. However, as the Stage Directions state, '*he stops himself*' (181) and instead banishes Cory to the other side of the fence. This scene concludes with Troy, alone, assuming a batting stance and commanding Death to pitch him ball. He is ready to do battle.

Act Two, Scene Five

Fences's last scene is about closure and forgiveness. It is now 1965, on the morning of Troy's funeral. Cory, now a military man, enters the yard and becomes reacquainted with his half-sister, Raynell. He also becomes acquainted with the truth of his reality, for after telling his mother that he does not plan to attend the funeral, he learns from her that, try as he might, he is very much like the father that ran him away. As she attempts to help Cory forgive Troy, Rose admits that while Troy had his faults, she allowed his wants and needs to consume her. Thus, she is just as much to blame for Troy's large sense of himself as he was. As the Maxson family and Bono have gathered to lay Troy's body to rest, they have also gathered within the fenced yard to lay Troy's sins to rest and forgive him. The drama concludes as Gabriel enters the yard and, as he promised, attempts to blow his horn to announce Troy's arrival at heaven's gates. After no sound emerges from the horn, Gabriel then dances as if possessed. This final action allows the presumed fool of the play to have the final word.

Character analysis

Troy Maxson

Troy Maxson is Wilson's penultimate 'everyman' character. James Earl Jones, who played the role of Troy Maxson in the play's Yale production through its last performance on Broadway, says of the character and Wilson's language: 'When I played Troy Maxson on Broadway in 1987, the speeches simply guided themselves' (2001: 84). It is these speeches that enable the audience to truly understand the magnitude and universality embodied by the character.

Troy is a man who is weighed down with responsibilities, but is determined to meet those responsibilities despite racism, economic inequality and illiteracy. Troy came into his manhood at 14, and by age 53, his age at the beginning of the play, he has survived and prevailed in a world that restricts the definitions of black manhood. He, in the jargon of his beloved baseball, 'bunted and proved them all wrong' (164), for he is married, has two sons (the older from his first marriage), a job and a home. Despite racism, Troy has succeeded after walking into the North and its American dream as best as an illiterate, African-American man can in the early part of the twentieth century. His strength lies within his hands, words and the desire to 'do right,' but Troy's strength and 'I ain't sorry for nothin' I done' (172) philosophy also present him as a selfish bully who wishes to control all those things and persons around him.

Rose Maxson

Rose Maxson's character states: 'But that's what life offered me in the way of being a woman and I took it' (190). This statement encapsulates her persona. Rose is a woman who allowed a 'big man' like Troy Maxson to mentally and physically consume her in exchange for protection against the external and internal challenges that many black women faced in the first five decades of the twentieth century. Rose loves Troy and strives to be the epitome of a good wife, despite the cost. Because of her willingness to sacrifice herself in order to be Troy's wife, Rose is often considered a strong, but underdeveloped representative feminist character. While I cannot completely counter this reading of Rose, I would expand the analysis to point out that Rose, especially after Troy admits to infidelity and refuses to stop his adultery, lets him know exactly how she feels. However, she does not leave Troy and, after the death of Troy's mistress, she raises his child as her own. Rose, the seeming antithesis to black feminist ideology, demonstrates her strong feminist voice when she tells Troy that from now on he is going to be a 'womanless man' (173). She chooses motherhood over marriage, and remains within the confines of the home that she has sacrificed herself to create for Cory, Troy, herself and now Raynell. Rose loves herself, but she loves her family also. Like many women in 1957, she made choices or rather sacrifices that reflected the choices/choicelessness that the world offered women, especially black women.

Gabriel Maxson

Gabriel Maxson is a Wilsonian spectacle character. Wilson explains these characters as 'mentally deficient' (Shannon, 1991: 143) and 'fully integrated into the other characters' lives, but they are a spectacle for the audience' (Lyons, 1997: 213). Gabriel's grand sense of himself may be misinterpreted as comic or even psychotic; however, he is just as strong as the other characters in this work. Gabriel is a war veteran, who has lost part of his brain for a country that still views him as a second-class citizen. Despite his handicap, he wants to be self-sufficient and respected as a man with his 'own key' (126). Gabriel once resided with the Maxsons, but he now lives independently in two rented rooms. An entrepreneur, Gabriel peddles second-hand fruit and vegetables in the Hill District and is proud of every quarter that he earns.

Gabriel's presence in this drama is two-fold, for not only does he serve as the spectacle character, but he also functions as the embodiment of a Greek chorus, moving the play's action along and providing a reminder to both the characters and the audience that a force exists that is greater than Troy Maxson.

Lyons Maxson

Lyons Maxson is probably the least developed of all of *Fences's* characters, but his flatness reflects his connection with, or rather disconnection from, his father. Lyons is the oldest Maxson child. He is a jazz musician, whose work ethic and musical taste contrast greatly with his father's. Troy Maxson is a blues man whose life has been filled with the blues' pains and pleasures. Lyons, in contrast, appears to posses a *carpe diem* attitude in which he chooses to create his own way and go against the established or accepted grain of black masculinity. He refuses to be controlled by life's strictures, and lives according to his own rules. Although Lyons's choices appear to be irresponsible in comparison to his father's choice, they are not less significant. Instead, they illustrate that Lyons, who was raised primarily by his mother, is very much his father's son. Like

Troy, he has created his own world view, and he will follow this view despite his father's or society's criticisms.

Cory Maxson

Cory Maxson is Troy Maxson's second child. He is the son who lives in Troy's home and eats Troy's food, and as his mother will remind him on the day of Troy's funeral, he is just like his father. Unlike his half-brother, Lyons, Cory has been reared in a nuclear family. He is a good student and athlete, and has a job at the local A&P. He is the direct recipient of Troy's fatherly instruction. Cory plays an integral role in *Fences* not only because he is the other half of the drama's father–son conflict, but also because he is the innocent half who is forced to accept his father's definition of responsibility. Cory's challenge in *Fences* is to leap over the fence of Troy so that he may find himself.

Raynell Maxson

Harry Elam, Jr offers a perfect reading of Raynell Maxson. He identifies her as being a ray of hope for the Maxson family:

> The seven-year-old Raynell, the product of Troy's illicit affair, enters in the final scene of *Fences* and produces powerful reverberations of change; she is the living manifestation of Troy's past infidelities and also the signifier of his eventual redemption. The intrusion of this new character during the play's denouement is a deliberate breach of the accepted conventions of realistic play construction. Wilson uses her appearance to convey the importance of legacy but also the potential for growth and progress. Significantly, Raynell's entrance not only occurs on the day of her father's funeral, but in the year 1965, in the midst of the Civil Rights era, a period of intense struggle and new opportunity for African Americans. Raynell's emergence at this precise moment brings a 'ray' of sunshine that hearkens a brighter tomorrow for the Maxson family and for black America. (Elam, 2004: 75)

I would like to expand Elam's reading of Raynell to show how Raynell is also a ray of hope for black womanhood. Rose realizes that she allowed Troy to consume her, and I suggest that Rose will (if this play's action were continued) raise Raynell to not only avoid the sins of her father, but also the self-inflicted sin that Rose committed against herself by giving up so much of herself in order to love someone else. I think it is significant that Raynell is a girl child, for up until his fifties Troy only sired sons. While Lyons does not share his work ethic or world view, and Cory is 'more like him' than he knows, Raynell brings Troy's transgressions full circle and, arguably, through her birth makes Troy realize the unique power that women possess, motherhood. He, unfortunately, does not live to see Raynell grow into womanhood, but he dies knowing that Raynell is being reared by Rose. Raynell has not only inherited Troy's blues song 'Old Blue', but has also been saved from a life of orphanage and illegitimacy through Rose's adoption of her. Rose is both Raynell's other mother and mama. She then, specifically, becomes Rose's ultimate ray of hope and second chance.

Jim Bono

Jim Bono is Troy Maxson's oldest friend and confidante. His friendship with Troy began, as with many of Wilson's protagonists, during their incarceration and lasts until he, along with Troy's family, sees Troy's corpse into the ground. Bono openly admires Troy's strength, boldness and resiliency; yet Bono, as a true friend should, does not shy away from his responsibility to point out Troy's faults and attempts to warn him to avoid those forces that could ruin the life that he has struggled to create. As disappointed by Troy's philandering as Rose is, Bono avoids Troy after he admits his affair, but he still cares for his friend. Bono is a true friend and, interestingly, he gets to hear Troy tell him that he loves him, something that Troy does not say to either of his sons during the course of the drama. Troy's words to Bono, 'I love you, nigger' (152), demonstrate the bond that black men can forge despite society's attempts to restrain, dehumanize and emasculate them. Bono's devotion to Troy and their friendship illustrates Wilson's particular perspective on African-American men as brothers, together, who can change their world.

Influences

Wilson composed *Fences's* first scene while riding on a bus, following *Ma Rainey's Black Bottom*'s success at the 1982 Eugene O'Neill Playwright's Conference (Herrington, 1998: 63). He wrote *Fences* in order to avoid the 'one play' trap that many African-American dramatists have succumbed to and to answer the critics' question (following the success of *Ma Rainey's Black Bottom*) of whether he could compose a 'traditional play' that focused primarily upon one character. According to Herrington, 'While his previous play, *Ma Rainey's Black Bottom*, achieved great critical and box-office success, it was faulted by many critics for its non-traditional structure and its bifurcated focus. Wilson reacted to the criticism as a direct challenge and strove to write a play with a conventional narrative, one large central character, and a more universal theme' (Herrington, 1998: 64).

Fences's critical and financial successes proved that Wilson, ever the warrior, met and exceeded the challenge. Through a realistic presentation of African-American lives, Wilson composed a drama that has become both a great American work and a universal work that is, as Herrington asserts, 'prime material for the study of the development of a playwright's vision for a single play' (Herrington, 1998: 77).

Fences illustrates Wilson's ability to navigate away from the ensemble style of *Ma Rainey's Black Bottom* and into a structure that would allow him to use a more traditional medium to relay the blues-filled story of Troy Maxson and the persons around him. However, while it may be argued that *Fences's* strongest influence was the traditional dramatic structure, the play was also influenced by an interdisciplinary collage of elements that included the artwork of Romare Bearden, the political and cultural rhetoric of Black Arts Movement dramatist Amiri Baraka (formerly Leroi Jones) and the African-American cultural soundtrack, the blues. Collectively, these influences reflect August Wilson, the cultural nationalist, and his allegiance to the beauty and survival of the African-American culture.

Romare Bearden's collage, *Continuities,* was the first component upon which Wilson based *Fences.* This image, featuring a man holding a baby in his arms, influenced the key scene where Troy returns to his yard holding baby Raynell and requests Rose's assistance to raise her. Wilson identifies *Fences's* next influence in several interviews, but he offers a full discussion in his 'The Ground on Which I Stand'. In this address, Wilson acknowledges his indebtedness to the artists of the 1960s Black Arts Movement:

> Ron Milner, Ed Bullins, Philip Hayes Dean, Richard Wesley, Lonne Elder III, Sonia Sanchez, Barbara Ann Teer and Amiri Baraka were among those playwrights who were particularly vocal and whose talent confirmed their presence in the society and altered the American Theater, its meaning, its craft, and its history. The brilliant explosion of black arts and letters of the 1960s remains, for me the hallmark and the signpost that points the way to our contemporary work on the same ground . . . (Wilson, 1997: 496)

Along with his contemporaries, Baraka provided Wilson with the cultural–political tools through which to excavate the complexity of Troy Maxson, the African-American Everyman. Wilson told David Savran that he 'liked' the language of Baraka's *Four Revolutionary Plays* and that he attempted to imitate Baraka in his earlier plays, but realized that he 'wasn't him and that wasn't going to work' (Sarvan, 1987: 23). He explained to Carl Rosen that Baraka's work influenced his through his 'ideas of black power, black nationalism' (1996: 199), and Herrington notes that in early drafts of *Fences*

Wilson had Troy express these types of communal convictions. As *Fences* evolved into its latter and final drafts, Troy became more selfish (Herrington, 1998: 74). This departure from Baraka illustrated Wilson's desire to find his own voice while, simultaneously, paying homage to the cultural–political 'kiln in which [he] was fired' (Wilson, 1997: 494).

The Blues, an African-American vernacular form that originated in Mississippi's Delta region at the beginning of the twentieth century, provided Wilson with the soundtrack through which to interpret and convey the meanings behind the African-American lives that he presented on stage. African-American blues musicians and singers originated and used the blues form to reflect the complexity and tragedy of disenfranchised, impoverished and segregated African-American life and to celebrate the ability of themselves and their people to survive despite and in the midst of life's challenges. After listening to his first blues recording, Wilson told Bill Moyers that this music altered his perspective. He began to truly understand the meaning of those stories that he would hear from the men who frequented the pool halls and restaurants where he worked during his twenties. Moreover, he began to recognize the significance of those unacknowledged African-American heroes and *she*roes who were the backbone of the African-American culture. Wilson stated:

> I began to see a value in the lives that I simply hadn't seen before. I discovered a beauty and nobility in their struggle to survive. I began to understand the fact that the avenues for participation in society were closed to these people and that their ambitions had been thwarted, whatever they may have been. The mere fact that they were still able to make this music was a testament to the resiliency of their spirit. (Moyers, 1988: 64)

Thus, 'Old Blue' becomes both Troy's survival testimony and eulogy as the audience hears him sing it during the course of the play, and then listen as his children – Cory and Raynell – perform it as a duet on the day of his funeral. The blues enabled Troy, specifically, and African Americans collectively, in the words of novelist and essayist Ralph Ellison, to 'keep the painful details and episodes of a brutal existence alive in one's aching consciousness, to finger its jagged grain, and to transcend it, not by consolation of philosophy but by squeezing from it a near-tragic, near-comic lyricism' (Ellison, 1964: 78) and to sing their songs for themselves.

Lastly and most importantly, *Fences* is greatly influenced by realism. In a 1999 interview with George Plimpton and Bonnie Lyons, Wilson expanded his list of dramatic influences to specifically include African-American novelists/playwrights/essayists Ed Bullins and James Baldwin. While Wilson had already referenced both men in other interviews, in this interview he states that in Bullins's work he 'first discovered someone writing plays about blacks with uncompromising honesty' (Plimpton and Lyons, 1999: 8). This same honesty not only greatly influenced Wilson's canon, but specifically *Fences*, in that Wilson realistically created a flawed hero and his family, a group of individuals that reflected every nuance of human existence honestly and realistically.

Close reading of key scenes

Fences is probably the most often anthologized of all of Wilson's dramas. One of the reasons for its popularity is its universally accessible themes of which the father–son conflict is central. When reading *Fences*, students are drawn deeply into the drama from its first act to its last, particularly as they begin to discover the man that is Troy Maxson.

Act One: 'I'm the boss around here'

If *Fences's* first act bore a title, it would be culled from Troy's words, 'I'm the boss around here' (135). In this first act, Troy evolves from being a lovable 'big man', who knows that he has rights and is willing to ask for them, into a human fence that not only seeks to construct the boundaries which his sons should traverse, but also a fence that no one or thing should attempt to cross. Troy, in essence, morphs into an extremely complex and brutally realistic man who may be difficult to love. Act One includes numerous moments that are imperative to understanding *Fences*, but there are several that reflect Wilson's dual tasks – to present the African-American culture honestly and to demonstrate the universality of the human experience.

As has been noted, one of *Fences's* main themes is father–son conflict. Troy's conflict is not with one, but with both his sons. The first conflict that arises is between Troy and Lyons. When Troy crosses a line and criticizes the way that Lyons has been raised by stating, 'Boy, your mama did a hell of job raising you' (120), Lyons quickly reminds Troy that he does not know how he was raised because he was not around (Troy was incarcerated) during his youth (120). This initial stand off is one that Troy, who is the boss, has to back down from because Lyons is correct. Troy cannot re-raise a 34-year-old man; he has missed this opportunity. Hence, he must accept Lyons for who he has become.

This act also presents probably the most memorable illustration of the father–son conflict when, in scene three, Cory asks Troy why is it that he 'ain't never liked' him? Innocently, Cory's question not only bears the weight of a child seeking approval from his parent, but also Cory's attempt to understand his father's actions. However, it is Troy's unsympathetic response that begins to mar his image in both the audience's eyes and Cory's. Instead of responding with a reassuring 'I like you,' Troy asks Cory, 'Who the hell say I got to like you?' (136), and explains to him that he and Rose are his responsibility and it is both his 'job' and 'responsibility' to provide for them, but liking him is not required (137). Troy is the atypical loving father in this scene, but the final words of this scene unveil the

fatherly advice and survival message that he attempts to relay to
Cory. This sage advice is what Troy learned from his father and on
his own but because of the harshness of the lessons he had to learn, he
does not possess a language through which to express this to his son.

It is not until the end of Act One that we discover the lesson
that Troy learned from his father. In this scene, Troy becomes a
sympathetic character who unfurls a past that is both brutal and
shocking. Through language, Wilson allows Troy to transport his
audience – Bono, Rose and Lyons – back into a time when Troy
was someone's innocent and vulnerable son. Troy relays the events
of his battle with his father, a battle that served as his rites of passage
ceremony from adolescence into manhood. In the course of this
ceremony, Troy physically challenged his father, lost the fight and
realized that, as he states, 'the time had come for me to leave my
daddy's house' (149).

Act One, Scene Four concludes with Troy serving as both umpire
and coach as he warns Cory that his rite of passage ceremony has
began. Using baseball jargon, his second language, Troy taunts Cory
by saying, 'You swung and you missed. That's strike one. Don't you
strike out!' (153). For many readers and audience members, especially males, this scene is eerily reflective of their own battles with
the fathers.

Act Two: The final showdown(s)

Fences's second act holds the final showdowns foreshadowed in Act
One. Just as a baseball player up to bat has three opportunities to
make contact with the leather-covered baseball before striking out,
and thus losing his opportunity to land on a base, Troy is served
three balls and strikes out once, twice and then a third time which,
symbolically, represents his death. Troy's first swing and miss is one
of the most important scenes in the entire play – his battle with
Rose. Students, especially female students, find this to be one of the
drama's most compelling, for it offers proof of Troy's selfishness and

Rose's strength. In Act One, Troy's cruel, but didactic, response to his son has already vilified him, but his announcement to his wife (of 18 years) that he has been having an affair, and that he and his lover are expecting a child, completes his vilification. In this scene Troy's selfishness surfaces, especially as he struggles to find the words to justify his infidelity. Rose is going through her daily ritual of taking care of her family members and preparing their dinner when Troy states, 'I'm trying to find a way to tell you . . . I'm gonna be a daddy' (161). Following this statement, Troy and Rose begin a sorrowful dramatic exchange in which she expresses her anger and disappointment, and he continues to defend his affair. Rose explains to Troy that she 'done tried to be everything a wife should be' for him, and that she hoped that their family would differ from her birth family, filled with half-brothers and sisters (162). Pleadingly she asks him the question 'why?', which is interestingly similar to Cory's question in the previous act, but, again, Troy fails to provide a redeeming response. Instead, he further buries himself within a moat of selfishness when he states that Alberta frees him from his familial responsibilities and enables him to be a 'different man' where he doesn't have to worry about bills or home repairs, but he can 'just be a part of [himself] that [he] ain't never been' (163). Moreover, when Rose asks Troy whether he plans to continue his relationship with Alberta, he does not hesitate to privilege his wants above his marital vows and declares that he cannot give up the euphoria that Alberta gives him.

This scene is also important because Troy resorts to baseball jargon to explain his affair. He becomes the announcer for a verbal baseball game in which he is the star player. Play by play, he announces how he has been able to make it from one base to the other without being tagged out. Rose and Cory were the first base, and Alberta 'firmed up his backbone' (164) and made him think that he could steal to second base. When Rose reminds him that their marriage is not a baseball game, Troy again struggles to explain himself and admits that he is in a state of ennui, and tired of staying on the same base of familial responsibility. During this exchange, Troy and Rose are supposed to be talking to each other, but Rose appears to be the only participant who is listening. While they both express important perspectives, Rose's voice usurps this scene especially as she explains to him how she has sacrificed her needs and wants to be his wife and helpmate and 'buried them inside' of him and their union (165).

In Act Two, Scene Three, which takes place 6 months after Troy's confession, he and Rose engage in a second battle that further establishes Rose as the nobler of the two. This scene also finds Troy attempting his second swing at the ball. In the previous scene, Troy learns that Alberta has died while giving birth to their daughter, Raynell. Troy confronts Death and challenges him to stay on the other side of the fence (that he wants to construct) so that he may protect those things and persons who belong to him until he is ready to face Death (170). Scene Three is set 3 days later. Troy returns to his yard carrying his motherless child and has to ask Rose for assistance:

ROSE. Okay, Troy . . . you're right. I'll take care of your baby for you . . . cause . . . like you say . . . she's innocent . . . and you can't visit the sins of the father upon the child. A motherless child has a hard time.

(*She takes the Baby from him.*)

From right now . . . this child got a mother. But you a woman-less man.

(*Rose turns and exits into the house with the Baby. Lights go down to black.*) (173)

Rose agrees to help Troy raise his child, but she dictates the terms of their relationship. Rose is in control, and Troy has struck out again. He has lost his wife and his mistress.

I have quoted Rose's speech in its entirety (and its accompanying stage directions) because it is one of the most powerful scenes in the play. This scene depicts an African-American male–female relationship that is, simultaneously, riddled with love and strife, and demonstrates Rose's strength and belief in the family unit, despite the 'sins of the father' and the head of the Maxson household. Moreover, this scene exemplifies the symbiotic relationship between Wilson's primary characters and the seemingly peripheral characters, the women. Thus, this scene is a battle won for black women, the black family unit, and Wilson, in that it presents a family that refuses to die and dissolve despite internal and external forces.

Troy makes his third strike in Act Two, Scene Four. Two months have passed, and a drunken, blues-singing Troy is sitting on the steps of the Maxson home. Cory attempts to climb the steps so that he may enter the house and tells his father, 'You in my way. I got to get by' (178). Cory's words mean much more than Troy is a physical obstruction. Troy is also a psychological barrier that has prevented Cory from growing into his own sense of manhood. Initially the action between Troy and Cory is primarily verbal, but Troy throws the first punch and shoves his son after Cory tells that he is just 'an old man' and he cannot be 'whup[ped]' by him anymore (180). This scene intensifies when Cory picks up Troy's bat and wields it as weapon of self-defence against his father. What ensues is a fierce battle of wills and repression as Cory and Troy, according to the stage directions '*struggle for the bat*' and then Troy, the father, the stronger of the two men, takes the bat, prepares to swing at his son, but instead of hitting his son, banishes Cory from 'around [his] house' (181). Finally, Cory is free, but the Maxson men's history repeats itself. Like his father, Cory has fought his father, lost, and has been made homeless by the father. It appears that Troy has won this battle, but Troy has struck out again. He has now lost Rose, Alberta and Cory.

Fences concludes in Act Two, Scene Five. This brief scene features two key moments that pay homage to the now deceased Troy. It is 8 years later, 1965, the American Civil Rights Movement has garnered victories against racialized school segregation in the South, Martin Luther King, Jr is the leader of a non-violent campaign to rid American of its racist practices, and Motown and Stax Records are providing rhythm and blues infused soundtracks for a slowly desegregating America. The blues has been incorporated into rhythm and blues, and Troy's body is on its way to the burial ground. However, Troy's blues song lives on.

Cory returns to the family home on the day of his father's funeral and becomes reacquainted with Raynell. Although the two barely know one another, they are linked by more than their father's blood and name; they also share his song. In what is *Fences's* most sentimental scene, Cory and Raynell perform the song 'Old Blue' as a duet, an action that proves that, despite Troy's actions, he attempted to be the best father that he could, and bequeathed his children an oral memory that they can share.

Act Two's final action centers upon Gabriel as he attempts to blow his horn as a signal to St Peter to open the gates for Troy's spirit. When the trumpet does not emit a sound, Gabriel does not give up. He begins what is described in the stage directions as '*a dance of atavistic signature and ritual*' and upon its conclusion remarks, 'That's the way that go!' (192). Gabriel refuses to allow anything to prevent him from announcing his brother's entry into heaven. Hence, the menacing Troy has been forgiven, and will find a home in the spiritual realm.

From beginning to end, *Fences* is a drama filled with scenes and speeches that mesmerize and encourage audiences to re-examine themselves and their families. *Fences* is a drama that summons all to recognize African-American men, their culture, and note the humanity and reality of their lives.

Changing views of the play

Fences has been an American dramatic masterpiece for almost a quarter of a century. From its first production at Yale to its most recent productions, it has earned and continues to earn primarily favorable reviews and lends itself to illuminating scholarly discussions. *Fences's* initial critiques were made by newspaper and magazine theatre critics. Shortly after the success of this great work and its predecessor, *Ma Rainey's Black Bottom*, August Wilson and *Fences* became recognized entities within academic circles. Thus, Wilson's back-to-back successes generated the first bio-critical discussion of *Fences* and his subsequent works, several collections of essays on the evolving Wilsonian dramatic canon, and, in this century, a published collection of interviews and a growing body of revisionist scholarship that is the result of Wilson's completed ten-play cycle. What follows are selected illustrations of the various journalistic and academic perspectives on *Fences*.

Fences received positive theatrical and scholarly reviews since its debut at the Yale Repertory Theatre in 1985. Following on the heels of *Ma Rainey's Black Bottom*'s success, *Fences*, as was to be expected, was often reviewed comparatively with this work, with most critics finding it to be a wonderful second work from a new Broadway name. Frank Rich, theatre critic for *The New York Times*, offered a balanced review of *Fences's* Yale production in which he compared the drama to *Ma Rainey's Black Bottom* and identified areas where the play failed, equaled, and exceeded its predecessor. Rich asserted that Wilson's play captures and presents the brewing racial strife of the 1960s. His achievement in the play is 'that he ma[de] us understand the father's behavior without ever sentimentalizing him,' and Rich praised Wilson's language and 'potent passages' (Rich, 1985) However, he also noted that *Fences* failed to properly acknowledge the strengths of the other characters, because Wilson 'worked so hard' to present a Troy whom audiences who could praise and despise. Rich suggested that:

> The reason for this shortfall in '*Fences*' may be that Mr Wilson has now learned more – may too much – about playwriting. '*Fences*' is technically better crafted than the previous work . . . But the dialogue doesn't always open up its speakers' hearts as the monologues in 'Ma Rainey' did . . . Similarly, the often splintery scenes seem designed to convey melodramatic story twists . . . rather than to chart the characters. (Rich, 1985; www. nytimes.com)

Two years later, after *Fences* had been substantially revised following productions at Yale and two regional theatres, *Fences's* production on Broadway compelled Brent Staples of *The New York Times* to laud Wilson's ability to reach several audiences with one play – men, women and a universal audience – and force him away from his 'comfortable . . . critical distance' and find himself 'among those for whom [*Fences*] is more than play' but also an opportunity to relive the experience of their own families, particularly their fathers. It is important to note that Staples recognized *Fences's* universality. He writes, 'Mr Wilson . . . has turned an interesting trick – he has found the universal in the particular without compromising the latter' (Staples, 1987). Moreover, Staples makes a compelling observation about *Fences's* effect on a black middle-class audience that reflects Wilson's 1960s Black Arts Movement influence and his identification of himself as both a black and cultural nationalist:

> Mr Wilson risks disapproval here – from black middle-class theatergoers who might resent what they perceive to be cultural dirty laundry washed in public, from white theatergoers who might feel on the outside of the proceedings . . . In effect, the

playwright has proceeded as if he don't give no nevermind about what middle-class folk think. So much the better here; because this play with virtually no concessions to the middle class has enfolded the universal in the particular, in a way that results in total accessibility – even if the audience response may not be typical for Broadway. (Staples, 1987)

Staples concludes his review of *Fences* with a poignant portrait of catharsis when he writes, 'and this son, third row center, seeing his father – work suit, rage, size and all – could only nod his head and think, "That's exactly how it was." He removed his glasses to reduce those two outlines colored in tears, and occasionally had to cover his eyes' (Staples, 1987). Hence, for Staples, an African-American theatre critic, Wilson accomplished his goal – to compose a drama that would prove that he could compose a 'traditional' drama, and that the African-American experience did and does reflect the entire human condition.

A third *New York Times* theatre critic called *Fences* 'the most powerful new American play of 1987' and applauded its ability to attract theatregoers who desired more than Broadway musicals and 'special effects' ('Stage View', 27 December 1987). This same critic credited Wilson with composing a drama that 'demand[s] that we think about who has what in American life' ('Stage View', 27 December 1987). *Time* magazine critic William A. Henry shared Rich's and Staple's favorable views of the play, and added that 'in craftsmanship, poignancy, and lingering impact, *Fences* represents a major step forward for Wilson' as a dramatist (Henry, 1987: 81). *Sports Illustrated* critic Robert W. Creamer's laudatory critique of *Fences* not only predicted that *Fences* was 'likely to become a classic staple of American drama' (Creamer, 1987: 13), but also noted the 'timelessness' of Troy's arguments about ageism and racism in the American baseball league(s) and the segregated duties of black and white garbage workers as the play, ironically, debuted shortly before American baseball found itself involved in another discussion of discrimination and desegregation.

While the majority of *Fences's* reviews were favorable, several critics found the drama to fall short. *The Nation's* Thomas Disch contended that *Fences* was 'less inspired than *Ma Rainey's Black Bottom*' and that the play's flaw was its focus on Troy Maxson who is the only person 'allowed to breathe' or rather really speak. Disch applauded James Earl Jones's performance, but found Wilson's words to be tantamount to 'spending an evening with a garrulous drunk' (Disch, 1987: 518).

In scholarly circles, Wilson's *Fences* has garnered and continues to evoke favorable acclaim and opportunities for study. Numerous scholars have penned books, chapters, essays and conference presentations that have interpreted *Fences* as not only Wilson's most conventional drama, but also the work that became the hallmark of his early commercial successes. Academically, *Fences* has been interpreted and discussed from historical, sociological, performative, black masculinist, feminist, black feminist and cultural perspectives, with most critics unanimously celebrating Wilson's brilliance. *Fences's* academic criticism has not changed drastically since its earliest discussions, but it has evolved with new Wilsonian scholars offering: (1) close revisions of the drama as part of Wilson's completed 10-play cycle; (2) more universal readings of the drama alongside the works of dramatists other than Eugene O'Neill, Arthur Miller and Tennessee Williams; and (3) more interdisciplinary readings of *Fences*. Thus, as any classic artistic work should, *Fences* will continue to generate new discussions in the decades to come.

Sandra Shannon composed one of the earliest scholarly discussions of Wilson's *Fences* in her book-length discussion of his early works, *The Dramatic Vision of August Wilson* (1995). In 'Developing Character: *Fences*, Shannon traces the play's conception and evolution from being a 'challenge' work to becoming Wilson's most lauded work. Within this discussion, Shannon discusses Wilson's maturation as a playwright and the evidence of this maturity in the complexity of the drama's anti-hero, Troy, and the cast of characters whose actions he – directly and indirectly – controls. Shannon contextualizes the drama not only within its specified post-World War II setting of 1957 and the decade of the 1950s, but she also biographically contextualizes *Fences's* central battle, what she terms the 'battle royal', between Troy Maxson and his son, Cory (and the first battle royal between Troy and the senior Mr Maxson, the sharecropper). Shannon asserts that this dramatic battle is reminiscent of Wilson's own battles with his stepfather, David Bedford, and his biological father and namesake, Frederick Kittel.

Shannon critically assesses the drama's other characters, but returns her focus to critically dissect Troy's character, his beliefs, sense of responsibility, grandeur and affinity for language. It is in the discussion of Troy's linguistic prowess that Shannon, once again, melds Troy and Wilson, for Wilson's abilities with language help to create *Fences* and the other nine works that comprise his dramatic canon as more than mere dramas, but works that hearken back and celebrate the complex beauty of the African-American oral tradition (Shannon, 1995: 104). Shannon discusses *Fences* comparatively with works composed by other African-American dramatists and Wilson's *Ma Rainey's Black Bottom*, *Joe Turner's Come and Gone* and *Jitney*.

In '*Fences*: The Sins of the Father . . .', Kim Pereira offers a compelling reading of the play's beginning and ending settings, 1957 and 1965, as he compares Troy to *Ma Rainey's* protagonist, Levee, and discusses the changing times. Pereira also offers an insightful discussion of *Fences's* separation theme, especially as it has effected and motivated the actions of the Maxson brothers – Troy and Gabriel (Pereira, 1995: 39).

Joan Herrington's *I Ain't Sorry for Nothin' I Done: August Wilson's Process of Playwrighting* (1998) offers a vital explanation of Wilson's early works – *Ma Rainey's Black Bottom, Jitney* and *Joe Turner's Come and Gone* – and a behind-the-scenes discussion of *Fences* from its beginnings at the O'Neill Center on through its Broadway debut. Herrington explains Wilson's playwriting process and shows the development of *Fences* through various drafts and its workshopped experiences. Specifically, Herrington asserts that, 'Because of its conventional structure and the streamlined nature of its character development, *Fences* is prime material for the study of the development of a playwright's vision for a single play' (Herrington, 1998: 77), and traces the evolution of Troy's character from being a 'Baraka-influenced' black nationalist 'to a more individualistic and more universal character' (Herrington, 1998: 74). Herrington's process reading of *Fences* dissects both the structure of the play and Wilson's dramatic perspective. Thus, her work technically grounds early readings of Wilson's *Fences* (and other works) and enables Wilson's scholar to further situate Wilson and Troy as dramatic engineers who, simultaneously, represent and construct a cultural icon.

Alan Nadel discusses *Fences* alongside Wilson's third commercial drama, *Joe Turner's Come and Gone*. Nadel offers a reading of *Fences's* titular fence as both a literal, inanimate object, and a metaphoric representation of American legal and racial boundaries. Nadel argues that *Fences* and *Joe Turner's Come and Gone* best illustrate Wilson's intention through his dramas and characters such as Troy to privilege their own meanings of humanity as they challenge the largely accepted American norms about race and privilege. In sum, Troy constructs his own meanings and encloses/protects them within his own person, and finally, within the space of his family's property.

Michael Awkward's contribution to *Fences's* scholarly canon interpreted the play (and its planned film adaptation) from an multi-theoretical perspective that included film, racial and cultural theories espoused by Omi, Winant, Clifford and Houston Baker, Jr. Awkward asserts that the play's artistic ancestry . . . is at least as much Euro-American as African, for the play's blues sensibilities (themselves an American invention) are figured in a text which displays its creator's obvious mastery of conventional Euro-American theatrical structure, pace, and methodology. Furthermore, its narrative events, particularly its exploration of family dynamics, appear – at least to me – intended self-consciously to recall, in particular, Arthur Miller's classic mid-twentieth century American drama, *Death of a Salesman*. (Awkward, 1994: 214)

As will be discussed in Chapter 3, Awkward's contentions expose a contradiction in *Fences* (the play) and in Wilson's demand that a black director be hired to direct the planned film adaptation. Moreover, Awkward joins the list of Wilson's critics who note the contradictions between Wilson the commercially successful playwright and Wilson the artist-activist, especially after his 1996 'The Ground on Which I Stand' address.

Craig Werner contributed to Wilsonian scholarship through highlighting jazz's influence and presence within Wilson's emerging canon. Largely the African-American oral forms presented in *Fences* are storytelling, blues, and lightly by way of Lyons, jazz. Werner's reading of *Fences* furthers the blues reading to include Wilson's blues woman – Rose – alongside the drama's blues men, and also reconfigures Gabriel, the spectacle character, as the embodiment of jazz in *Fences*. Werner writes that Gabriel 'combines the blues and gospel dimensions of the jazz impulse' (Werner, 1994: 41) especially as he attempts to announce Troy's presence at heaven's gates by first blowing into a mouthpiece-less horn, but then breaking into a dance and finally a howl. Gabriel – the person and his actions – become a human site of 'fragmentation' and, according to Werner, 'Wilson bears witness to Gabriel's jazz vision, his burden and his call' (Werner, 1994: 42).

More recently, Harry J. Elam, Jr ushered in new discussions of not only *Fences* and its characters, but also Wilson's evolving dramatic cycle with the publication of *The Past as Present in the Drama of August Wilson*. In this text, Elam examines Wilson's manipulation of time within his dramatic cycle and argues that 'Wilson's history cycle reveals an African-American continuum that is always in process, stretching back into Africa and reaching into the future' (Elam, 2004: xix). Elam offers compelling discussions of Rose Maxson as both a mother and wife, Gabriel Maxson along with his kin (Wilson's other spectacle characters), and Troy and Wilson's other male characters illustrating Wilson's aim to 'represent black masculinity so that it becomes a site of self-determination, pride, self-respect, and historical consciousness' (Elam, 2004: 128).

In Staging Masculinity: Male Identity in Contemporary American Drama, Carla McDonough turns the focus specifically to Troy Maxson and argues that *Fences* is 'ultimately the story of manhood as measured against that illusory American dream of material gain, only this time the struggles of the male protagonist are further heightened by questions of racism' (McDonough, 1997: 147). McDonough compares *Fences* and Troy Maxson to their white American counterparts, *Death of a Salesman* and Willy Loman, and suggests that like Loman for whites, Troy's character becomes representative of the 'black experience in America'. Moreover, McDonough makes a strong argument when she asserts that much of Troy's 'power' is, like that of Hansberry's Walter Lee Younger, enabled because of the black women (in *Fences* Rose and Alberta), who support them (McDonough, 1997: 149).

McDonough's discussion of *Fences* and Troy is especially important because she discusses *Fences* alongside Wilson's *Joe Turner's Come and Gone* and *The Piano Lesson*, but within a text that comparatively examines images of masculinity dramatized in the works of dramatists Sam Shepard, David Mamet and David Rabe. She contends that these works have oftentimes overlooked the connection between 'race and issues of masscult' (McDonough, 1997: 136). Wilson's works, however, provide 'excellent texts for reading how race as well as gender factor into male conflicts with and struggles for normative masculinity' (McDonough, 1997: 137).

Peter Wolfe's discussion of *Fences*, 'The House of Maxson', offers a celebratory but critical reading of *Fences's* protagonist, Troy Maxson, and applauds Wilson's ability to create such a complex and tragically flawed character with whom audiences could and did empathize. Wolfe's discussion of *Fences* also identities the drama's embedded coding of and connection to Troy's beloved sport, baseball. While Wilson, the play, and many scholars and critics address Troy's participation in the Negro Baseball League and his frustration because he was too old to pursue baseball as his career, Wolfe is one of a few to note how Wilson further strengthens Troy's connection to baseball as he identifies the numerous 'coincidental' intersections between baseball history and statistics, the play's production history, and its characters (Wolfe, 1999: 56–57).

Twenty-first century scholarship on the drama began with Anna Blumenthal offering a new reading of *Fences* in that she re-focuses attention on *Fences's* orality through Troy's storytelling. Blumenthal asserts that while early scholarship on *Fences* acknowledges Troy's gift of storytelling as a component of the African-American oral tradition and as Wilson's illustration of the African-American culture, few scholars have studied the use and performative characteristics of Troy's story. Blumenthal's scholarship suggests that Troy's character is not only the nucleus of *Fences* because Wilson has intentionally created a character-driven play, but also because Troy's character is able to create and control an audience that will aurally witness his verbal performances and, hopefully, learn from them. Hence, Troy Maxson becomes an African-American griot who 'enacts paternal and familial duty by teaching it in his narrative' (Blumenthal, 2000: 80).

3 Production History

This chapter offers a brief history of American theatre productions of *Fences*. It also discusses Margaret Booker's production of *Fences* in Beijing, China in 2000, the 2006 production of *Fences* at the Pasadena Playhouse (Pasadena, California), the controversial and yet-to-be-filmed filmic adaptation of the play, and the Kennedy Center's spring 2008 staged reading production.

Following in the footsteps of *Ma Rainey's Black Bottom*, Wilson submitted *Fences* to the Eugene O'Neill Theater Center's 1983 National Playwright's Conference. The play was accepted and presented as a staged reading at this conference. Herrington details how Wilson, *Fences* and Wilson's latter plays benefited from his repeat performances at the O'Neill Conference (1982, *Ma Rainey's Black Bottom*; 1983, *Fences*; 1984, *Joe Turner's Come and Gone*; 1986, *The Piano Lesson*, 1991 Wilson's dramaturge year; and 1994, *Seven Guitars*), and outlines how *Fences* evolved from Wilson's original text to its Broadway version. Following the O'Neill's Pre-Conference (the first time the selected playwrights meet and read their plays aloud and are assigned a director and dramaturge), Wilson altered the structure of *Fences* from being relayed in flashback to a chronological plot. Wilson then revised the drama again during the summer portion of conference in which the plays are presented as staged readings to two different audiences (the conference participants and staff, and the public). Herrington states that between the two readings, Wilson cut 'forty-five minutes from the play' (1998: 53).

Lloyd Richards, again, took the directorial helm of an August Wilson work and *Fences* moved from the O'Neill Playwright's Conference to the Yale Repertory Theatre in New Haven, Connecticut. The play opened there on April 30, 1985. The original cast included James Earl Jones as Troy Maxson, Mary Alice in the role of Rose Maxson, Courtney B. Vance played the role of Cory Maxson, Raynell Maxson was played by Cristal Coleman and LaJara Henderson, Charles Brown portrayed Lyons, Russell Costen starred in the role of Gabriel Maxson and Ray Aranha performed the role of Jim Bono. Before its Broadway debut, *Fences* took what Jeremy Gerard called 'A Productive Detour' (Gerard, 1987) and continued to follow the path Wilson's works from *Ma Rainey's Black Bottom* on through the final work, *Radio Golf,* would journey (through a succession of regional theatres and then Broadway). This Yale-Regional theatre-Broadway trajectory enabled Wilson to utilize a unique production and revision process for his plays which proved beneficial as he continued to compose his twentieth-century cycle of plays.

Regional productions

Fences migrated from the Eugene O'Neill Center's Playwright's conference to Yale's stage, and then to the Goodman Theatre in Chicago, Illinois, in January 1986. The Goodman's production of *Fences* offered Wilson a new space from which to revise the play and correct some of its early flaws. For example, Wilson told Gerard that the Goodman staging was 'very helpful . . . especially with the same cast and production team. At Yale, there were long blackouts between the scenes because James Earl Jones would have to have a costume change between the end of one scene and the beginning of the next. We eliminated them by writing bridges between the scenes (Gerard, 1987). Moreover, *Fences* forged a collaboration between Wilson and the Goodman Theatre that proved beneficial for both participants. Wilson found the first of several regional spaces in which to perfect his work, the Goodman Theatre is one of the few theatres that has produced all 10 of August Wilson's plays, and because of its partnership with Wilson, the theatre has diversified its audience and 'since *Fences* . . . presented more than 20 [twenty] plays by other African-American writers' (Goodman Theatre's website, 2007 at www.goodmantheatre.org). Thus, *Fences* began a collaborative process that Wilson's latter works also followed: pre-Broadway stagings at regional theatres that allowed him to test out early versions of the plays.

At the close of the Goodman's production of *Fences*, the production rights were purchased by Carole Shorenstein Hays and *Fences* had its first commercial staging in San Francisco, California, but not before a Seattle, Washington production at the Seattle Repertory Theatre (1985–1986 season) featuring a different cast. Wilson also forged a bond with the Seattle Repertory Theatre, and like the Goodman Theatre, it has produced all of Wilson's plays. The most recent production was the 2007 production of *Gem of the Ocean*, directed by stage, screen, television, and Wilsonian actor, Phylicia Rashad.

Fences on Broadway

Finally, 4 years following its initial staged reading *Fences* debuted on March 26, 1987, on Broadway, at the 46th Street Theatre. The production was directed by Lloyd Richard and featured most of the original cast members, with the exception of Gabriel played by Frankie R. Faison and Karima Miller in the role of Raynell. *Fences* ran at the 46th Street Theatre for 525 performances from March 26, 1987 to June 26, 1988, garnering Tony Awards for Best Play, Best Direction of a Play (Lloyd Richards), Best Actor in a Play (James Earl Jones), Best Featured Actress in a Play (Mary Alice); the Pulitzer Prize for Drama, Drama Desk Awards for Outstanding New Play,

Outstanding Actor in a Play (James Earl Jones), and Outstanding Featured Actress in a Play (Mary Alice). The play grossed 11 million dollars.

Recent productions

Since Wilson's death in 2005, numerous productions of his plays have taken place throughout the country. In American regional and university theatres, Wilson's words have inspired and moved audiences. From the Yellow Brick Studio in Honolulu, Hawaii to Jackson State University's (located in Jackson, Mississippi) September 2007 production, to Princeton University (Princeton, New Jersey) and Delaware State University (Dover, Delaware), audiences have responded to *Fences* and Wilson's other moving dramas of African-American life.

One of the most highly anticipated productions of the play debuted in September 2006, when Wilsonian alumni Angela Bassett and Laurence Fishburne headlined in the Pasadena Playhouse's revival of *Fences*. Directed by Sheldon Epps, this powerful version continued the national productions of Wilson's works, and afforded Bassett and Fishburne the opportunity to work together on a play. Bassett acted in role of Martha Pentacost in Wilson's *Joe Turner's Come and Gone* at both the Yale Repertory Theatre (1986 and 1987) and at Broadway's Ethel Barrymore Theatre, and Fishburne acted the role of Sterling Johnson in *Two Trains Running* (for which he won a Tony Award). Basset told Gia Gittleson, 'When [the film] *Akeelah and the Bee* opened, Laurence and I talked about *Fences*. Then Sheldon Epps, the artistic director at the Pasadena Playhouse, asked me, 'We've got the rights to *Fences*. Do you have any interest?' I thought, 'My gosh, you heard our private conversation!' (Gittleson, 2006: 230). Hence, *Fences* was re-born.

Garnering favorable reviews, this production featured Bassett in the role of Rose, Fishburne, in the role of Troy, Wendell Pierce played Jim Bono, Lyons was played by Kadeem Hardison, Raynell was played by Victoria Matthews, Bryan Clark reprised Cory and Gabriel was portrayed by Orlando Jones. Robert Verini writes of the universality of *Fences* and Epps's revival of the drama, 'It is specific enough to act as a cornerstone of Wilson's ten-play Pittsburgh Cycle, yet universal enough to touch a chord in every human heart' (Verini, 2006: 61). Particularly he noted the merits of Fishburne's and the other male cast members' performances:

> Fishburne may be less terrifying a figure than the original Troy, James Earl Jones, but he is a more recognizable Everyman. . . .
> Utterly real throughout are the men of the household, each of whom Wilson uses to embody a different vision of how one may approach life. Kadeem Hardison is definitive as Troy's older son Lyons . . . Clark avoids whininess as Cory. . . . But the real acting surprise is Orlando Jones as Troy's war-wounded brother, who now believes he is the Archangel Gabriel. Unhampered by this symbolic baggage, Jones demonstrates an intensity and emotional accessibility hitherto unhinted at. (Verini, 2006: 61)

The title of the Pasadena Playhouse's July 2006 Press Release announcing this production read, 'A Landmark Event In the American Theatre', and Epps summed up the sentiments of many *Fences* directors, especially as they produced commemorative productions of *Fences* and Wilson's other works in the period following his demise: 'This is our way of honoring August . . . *Fences* is one of my favorite plays and what a wonderful way to introduce Playhouse audiences to his work that [sic] with this, his most powerful and profound piece. *Fences* is a beautifully written play . . .' ('A Landmark Event . . .,' 2006).

Fences made its next national presentation in Washington, DC, at The John F. Kennedy Center for Performing Arts in March

2008. Directed by Wilsonian actor and director Kenny Leon, this production was the fifth work presented as part of the Kennedy Center's August Wilson's twentieth Century Theatrical Series, in which each of Wilson's 10 plays were produced, chronologically, as staged readings beginning with *Gem of the Ocean*, set in 1904, and concluding with *Radio Golf*, set in the 1990s.

International productions

The American universality of *Fences* had been tested and confirmed by the time of its final Broadway curtain call, and in the 1990s, its international universality would test its cross cultural translatability. In 1996, scholar-director Margaret Booker took *Fences* to the East, Beijing, China, and presented the work at the National Theatre of China where 'not one actor had been to America, knew an African-American, or even spoke English' (Booker, 1997: 50). This production challenged Wilson's condemnation of color-blind casting as presented in the (in)famous 'The Ground on Which I Stand' speech presented at the 1996 Theatre Communications Group meeting and as Booker notes, as she quotes Wilson: '. . . testifies to his belief that he writes about issues common to all cultures, but roots them in the black experience' (Booker, 1997: 51).

On the issue of color-blind casting Wilson stated:

Colorblind casting is an aberrant idea that has never had any validity other than as a tool of the Cultural Imperialist who views their American Culture, rooted in the icons of European Culture, as beyond reproach in its perfection. . . . The idea of colorblind casting is the same idea of assimilation that black Americans have been rejecting for the past 380 years. For the record we reject it again. We reject any attempt to blot us out, to reinvent history and ignore our presence or to maim our spiritual product. (Wilson, 1997: 498–99)

However, Booker's production of _Fences_ appears to have offered a compromise to color-blind casting because the actors did not attempt to assume and imitate black people or black culture, but they were allowed to locate _Fences's_ shared connections with their own Chinese culture and act on these connections. Despite anticipated cultural 'clashes,' _Fences's_ eastern debut was a resounding success for everyone involved in and witnessing the production. Booker, Wilson and Liu Jinyuan, the director of the Beijing People's Art Theatre, recognized the universal and human connections that _Fences_ plot identified (Booker, 1997: 50) and production began on a play that would later edu-tain patrons who would '[ride]ing bicycles one-and-one-half hours to get there (and the same time to return home),' and pay '20 to 50 yuan for a ticket on an average salary of 400 yuan per month' (Booker, 1997: 51).

Before _Fences_ was ready for its Chinese production, several stereotypes had to be challenged and cultural compromises would have to be met. As with any production, the director had to instruct the cast on the drama – context, character motivations, dialect, language, etc.; however, Booker's task was especially daunting because she had to perform '[t]he trick' of 'tak[ing] something essentially African-American and transform[ing] it into something emotionally meaningful for the Chinese' (Booker, 1997: 51). Using _The Piano Lesson_ (the only drama adapted into film), 'American films, sports videos, and blues music, and five days of thorough text work,' Booker and the cast attempted to 'capture the colloquialisms, rhythm and poetry of the dialogue, and occasionally adjusted parts of the translation to capture Wilson's style and meaning' (Booker, 1997: 51). Once mastered, the production was faced with the dilemma of how to transform a Chinese actor into a black character, physically. Booker explains this discussion:

> The company, used to transforming themselves into foreigners through wigs and makeup, were concerned about pretending to

be African American. Liang Guanhua, who played Troy, said, 'When we first started, we thought we'd have to paint ourselves black, but the director said "No!" I did not want black-faced caricatures of these very real people, but wanted the actors to think of their characters as themselves. (Booker, 1997: 52)

Booker's decision to avoid both black face minstrelsy and cultural minstrelsy proved favorable and garnered praise from Beijing critics and Mike Laris of the *Washington Post* who found the play to be 'an endearing combination of 1950s Pittsburgh and 1990s Beijing' (as quoted by Booker, 1997: 52). Xie Xizhang of the *Beijing Evening News* wrote of the play, 'By the end you feel connected with black people's destiny. The problems Troy and his family face are very much like those faced by average people in China' (Booker, 1997: 52).

This production as Booker notes, and I concur, also proves the interconnectedness between the folk of Beijing and the African-American folk that Wilson's works celebrate and excavate. Booker writes of Beijing: 'Rushing toward the 21st century on a rampage of consumerism, China in the 90s wants to be a member of the modern world and economic community, yet still tries to preserve its intellectual tradition and social values. Nowhere would the clash between old and new be more apparent' (Booker, 1997: 50). Immediately, this description brings forward the cultural clashes – inter and intra – that take place within Wilson's *Fences*. Lyons's jazz culture collides with Troy's Blues culture; Troy's patrilineal teachings collide with Cory's new-generational needs; Rose's gynocentric perspectives challenge Troy's masculinist philosophies; and, simply, the old ways collide with new. Liu, according to Booker, identifies these chasms in China as a 'generation ditch' and Wilson identifies this as the loss of one's song. Despite the cultural differences (which, though important, were few) Booker and the National Theatre of China were able to accomplish much more than recreating the Pittsburgh Hill District on a Chinese stage. Instead they were able to identify 'parallels with old Beijing's hutongs surrounded by modern construction and factories' and Troy's home in the Hill District, and enable 'Beijing's older generation – veterans of the early days of the People's Republic, famine and political changes – [to find] their counterparts in the Maxson family. The story of an illiterate black garbage collector who had moved to industrial Pittsburgh to create a better life made lots of sense in Beijing where former farmers clean the streets so their sons and daughters can attend university' (Booker, 1997: 51).

Booker's *Fences* broke down cultural fences and tilled a new ground for Wilson's work. She even quotes Wilson saying: 'There are some things specific to human life being lived as a black man in America . . . but there is no idea that cannot be contained by that. It's different than as a Chinese man in China, but damn if we don't all know a betrayal when we see one. We all have conflicts with our parents' (Booker, 1997: 52).

Fences has also been staged in Ghana, West Africa. Wilson explained to Shannon and Williams that one of the differences in this production was that Gabriel was moved into a more Greek influenced choral position, where he would 'speak directly to the audience' (Williams and Shannon, 2004: 194). Also, according to Charles Mulekwa, three of Wilson's works including *Fences* in 1988, had been produced in Uganda, Africa. Mulekwa states that *Fences's* language 'was considerably different from what we were accustomed to, but the dramatic quality of human aspirations and the struggle to be human in the face of other people, were so resonant' (www.earthtimes.org Monday, 3 October 2005).

From page to stage, from stage to screen? – The Filmic Translation of August Wilson's *Fences*

Fences earned August Wilson numerous awards, solidified his presence on Broadway, and began to secure him the title of one of

America's greatest playwrights.. However, the controversy surrounding this drama's planned film adaptation also revealed and reminded Wilson's supporters, dramatic scholars and critics that Wilson was, first and foremost, 'a race man'. In 1987, Paramount Pictures purchased the rights to create a filmic adaptation of *Fences* for $500,000 that would be produced by and star comedian-actor Eddie Murphy in the role of Lyons. Eddie Murphy's name, like James Earl Jones's on the marquee of the theatre, would assure Paramount a wide and diverse audience, but little did Murphy or the studio anticipate August Wilson's powerful protection of the cultural integrity of his work.

Wilson began composing the screenplay in 1989, but the production was already mired in debate because Wilson preferred that the studio hire a black director to oversee the adaptation. This request placed Wilson and the studio (and Murphy) at odds, especially because Paramount had already identified a director for the film – Barry Levinson. However, Levinson did not meet Wilson's criteria. In the opinion piece, 'I Want a Black Director' Wilson clearly articulates his reasons for preventing Paramount from adapting *Fences* without the directorial perspective of a black director:

> When they had lined up Barry Levinson . . . I met with Barry. Barry wanted to do the film, so I went over [to] Paramount's office and said, 'I don't want Barry to do the film. He doesn't qualify'. A qualification was that the director had to be black, that he have some sensibilities to the culture.
>
> This is a drama about the culture. And in these instances, I think you should hire . . . if this were a film about Italian culture, you should hire an Italian director. This is common sense. Now, if you have an adventure movie that's not specific to a particular culture, you can hire anybody to direct that. (Wilson, 1994)

In order to assist Paramount in fulfilling his request, James Greenberg writes that Wilson and his attorney John Breglio submitted a list of potential candidates for the position that included Spike Lee, Lloyd Richards, Gordon Parks and Charles Burnett; and later Warrington Hudlin (then president of the Black Film Makers' Foundation), and at Mr Breglio's request, compiled a second list of 12 additional candidates for the job (Greenberg, 1991: 2–3). As of January 1991, Greenberg stated that Bill Duke was the 'front runner for the job'; however, *Fences* has yet to appear on the big screen. According to Mary Ellen Snodgrass, Wilson had completed the final draft of *Fences's* screenplay in 2003. Interestingly, this adaptation removed Alberta, Troy's mistress, from the shadows and gave her a speaking role in the work, and Wilson had begun to cast the filmic adaptation himself with Marion McClinton as director, Alfre Woodard as Rose, and Oprah Winfrey in the role of Alberta (Snodgrass, 2004: 19).

While Wilson offers a compelling argument in 'I Want a Black Director' that is consistent with the cultural–political position presented in the 'The Ground on Which I Stand' speech delivered at the 1996 Theatre Communications Group meeting, scholar Michael Awkward offers an enlightening critique of the gaps in Wilson's logic that cause his demand for a black director to be both contradictory to his accomplishments as a black playwright whose success has largely come from white theatre patrons. Awkward's critique of the play and his response to Wilson's call for a black director illustrates just one of the responses to Wilson's request. Germane to Awkward's argument is that Wilson's requirement that *Fences's* director be black is a complicated one because his argument excludes both non-black and non-black identifying blacks from consideration. Moreover, Awkward asserts that Wilson's position contradicts the reality of American cultural exchange:

> But his argument is weakened, in my view, by his efforts to polarize white and black means of access to Euro-American and 'foreign' (in this case, black) cultural production. The problem is

not that his exploration of traditional caucacentric perspectives on black art is unpersuasive but rather that he suggests, despite the technological advances that have made possible a wider dissemination of black cultural material, that an Afro-American ethos remains inherently less available to a white interpreter than, say, the aesthetics of Euro-American drama are to a black American such as himself. (1994: 213)

Awkward's point is interesting and illustrates the inherent complexity of August Wilson's cultural perspective and dramatic vision, especially as it supports Wilson's position against color-blind casting, but challenges the overarching universality of his works. However, while I support Wilson's desire to preserve cultural authenticity for his work and what I identify as his way to remind the 'powers that be' that talented and qualified African-American film directors do and have existed, Awkward's argument demands that closer examinations of the concept of cultural ownership take place so that American theatrical and filmic discussions may become truly universal entities. Most importantly, Awkward's position illustrates Wilson's ability, through his work and his words, to raise important questions concerning the true state of American culture.

Fences, the drama, became Wilson's 'Everyman' play for the Broadway stage. Paramount Pictures probably banked on *Fences*, the film, as being another film that would illustrate its appreciation of diversity and its desire to move toward presenting more ameliorative images of black life. For Wilson, then, to prevent the play's adaptation appears to be a counteractive movement to align Americans and American dramatists on a 'common ground' (Wilson, 1996: 502), but I suggest that actors, audiences, scholars, critics and teachers reconsider Wilson's over-protectiveness of his drama and appreciate the cultural baggage that he has brought along with him into the theatre world. Wilson's biographical information sheds insight into the life of a man who faced racism head on within the

American educational system, who heard the tales of black southern life from his poolroom professors and, when on the road to success, 'almost' fell victim to forces that wanted him to transform *Ma Rainey's Black Bottom* from a drama into a musical. Hence, by the time Paramount optioned *Fences,* Wilson had already been introduced to non-African-American conceptualizations of his work, and appears to have decided that he must protect the sanctity of his vision.

The *Fences* saga began in 1987, but the film adaptation has yet to be made. In the end, Wilson has been able to protect his dramatic vision until Paramount chooses to honor his request to hire a black director for the project. Fortunately, one August Wilson work has been adapted into film. In 1995, Wilson's *The Piano Lesson* was presented on CBS's Hallmark Hall of Fame. Wilson authored the screenplay and his friend and director Marion McClinton, an African-American director, directed the production. It is interesting that CBS allowed Wilson's ownership and artistic control of this piece, but Paramount Pictures could not, initially, understand his need to tell his story and sing his song in his own way.

4 Workshopping the Play

This chapter offers a series of practical workshop exercises based on *Fences*. It involves discussion of the play's characters, conflicts, key scenes, motifs and ideas which a group of student actors could explore. The content is also informed by interviews with actors and directors who have been involved in professional productions of the play.

The world of *Fences*: a contextual approach

Fences offers a glance back in time to the years preceding the 1960s and the American Civil Rights movement. It addresses the continued complexities of (specifically) a black man and (generally) a people, who both have managed to survive slavery, sharecropping, disenfranchisement and racial segregation. *Fences*, however, is a fiction, a didactic fiction. It is not an historical piece, but rather a piece that uses history as its foundation as it presents a multifaceted examination of various -isms that plagued and continue to plague both the black man and black culture. *Fences* affords actors and students the opportunity to travel back into the lives of their parents, grandparents and great-grandparents to begin to understand the importance of knowing and reconnecting one's self to one's history, a lesson that August Wilson emphasized in his twentieth-century cycle of plays.

Visualization

Actors should be immersed in *Fences*'s world through various forms of media. In order to begin to understand the history of Troy Maxson's character as the son of a sharecropper, actors should, as a group, view historical videos and documentaries that present images of the South and the Great Migration. The Blackside Film and Video production company's award winning *Eyes on the Prize: America's Civil Rights Movement 1954–1985* and the WGBH-produced *Reconstruction: The Second Civil War* offer historical discussions of the America that the ancestors of *Fences's* characters called home, and serve as moving contexts through which to interpret Troy's anger, Rose's determination, and a means to understand the significance of Troy's request that he be allowed to drive the rubbish truck instead of riding on back. In order to understand more fully how and why African Americans migrated from the South to the North, actors should visit 'In Motion: The African-American Migration Experience' at The Schomburg Center for Research in Black Culture's website (http://www.inmotionaame.org/migrations/landing.cfm?migration=8&bhcp=1). This site provides statistical information, photographs and primary source documents that serve as a record of the number of Africans Americans who, like Troy, found their way to the North.

A less historical, but more popular culture influenced visualization exercise could be a contrast of *Fences's* setting and characters with the 1950s set American situation comedy *Happy Days*. This program, which ran on American television from 1974 to 1984, centered on the angst of white American middle-class teenagers and their 'leader' Fonzie, a working-class renegade. I can recall one episode where the comedy's lead character, Richie Cunningham, and his family have to deal with the complexities of an African-American family moving into their neighborhood, but the program's white, Milwaukee, Wisconsin-based world sits in direct contrast to the Pittsburgh, Pennsylvania Hill District where Troy fights to raise his family. It is through this contrast that the actors may begin to understand or decry Wilson's focus on black culture as a specific and unique culture, and trouble his focus to note that despite race, any American who does not fit into the mainstream or rather privileged class, for example like Fonzie, finds it difficult to assimilate into a hegemonic ideal.

Numerous visuals will enable actors to begin to understand *Fences's* world, but actors should also experience this world aurally – through African-American music and folklore. Actors should study the musical genre blues either beginning with Bessie Smith's 'Nobody Can Bake a Sweet Jelly Roll Like Mine', which was one of Wilson's initial influences for his dramatic cycle, or listening to recordings of Mississippi Blues singers such as Robert Johnson and Muddy Waters. Blues songs are not main characters in *Fences*, as they were in *Ma Rainey's Black Bottom*, but Troy's song, 'Old Blue', is both his song and his legacy to his children. Actors should be asked to listen to the stories relayed in the blues songs selected and note their rhythms and patterns. Then, each actor should either sing Troy's song individually or in pairs in order to workshop Raynell and Cory's duet in the play's last scene and experience the bond that this blues song creates between Troy's children, between Troy and his children and, if performed correctly, between Troy and the audience.

Reading *Fences*: the ground on which Wilson stands

Before actors can effectively workshop *Fences*, they must first understand the drama's culture and the dramatist's perspective. The didactic approach suggested in the previous section of this chapter will enable actors to begin to understand the historical period in which the play's plot unfolds, but in order to understand Wilson's perspective, actors must study Wilson's dramatic manifesto –'The Ground on Which I Stand'.

'The Ground on Which I Stand' is the keynote address that Wilson delivered at the 1996 Theatre Communications Group meeting.

In this address, Wilson first identifies and pays homage to both his cultural and dramatic ancestors:

> In one guise the ground I stand on has been pioneered by the Greek dramatists, by Euripides, Aeschylus and Sophocles, by William Shakespeare, by Shaw and Ibsen, and by the American dramatists Eugene O'Neill, Arthur Miller and Tennessee Williams. In another guise the ground that I stand on has been pioneered by my grandfather, by Nat Turner, Denmark Vesey, by Martin Delaney, Marcus Garvey and the Honorable Elijah Muhammad. That is the ground of the affirmation of the value of one being, an affirmation of his worth in the face of the society's urgent and sometimes profound denial. It was this ground as a young man coming into manhood, searching for something to which to dedicate my life, that I discovered in the Black Power movement of the 1960s. (Wilson, 1997: 493–94)

Wilson then asserts that he is a 'race man': 'That is simply that I believe that race matters. That is the largest, most identifiable, and most important part of our personality. It is the largest category of identification because it is the one that most influences your perception of yourself, and it is the one to which others in the world of men most respond' (Wilson, 1997: 494). This speech takes an interesting turn when Wilson begins to challenge the practice of color-blind casting and equates it with almost four centuries of African-American 'assimilation' (Wilson, 1997: 498):

> To mount an all black production of *Death of a Salesman* or any other play conceived for white actors as an investigation of the human condition through the specific of white culture is to deny us our own humanity, our own history, and the need to make our own investigations from the cultural ground on which we

stand as black Americans. It is an assault on our presence, our difficult but honorable history in America, and an insult to our intelligence, our playwrights, and our many and varied contributions to the society and the world at large. The idea of colorblind casting is the same idea of assimilation that black Americans have been rejecting for the past 380 years. For the record we reject it again. We reject any attempt to blot us out, to reinvent history and ignore our presence or to maim our spiritual product. . . . We do not need colorblind casting. We need some theaters to develop our playwrights. (Wilson, 1997: 499)

Wilson's address, after indicting American funding agencies for ignoring and under-subsidizing black theatre companies and playwrights, closes with a unifying thought and tone that 'together' black and white American theatre practitioners may correct past wrongs and support black theatre in the manner that it should have been:

The ground together. We have to do it together. We cannot permit our lives to waste away, our talents unchallenged. We cannot permit a failure to our duty. We are brave and we are boisterous, our mettle is proven, and we are dedicated.

The ground together. The ground of the American theater on which I am proud to stand . . . the ground which our artistic ancestors purchased with their endeavors . . . with their pursuit of the American spirit and its ideals. (Wilson, 1997: 503)

Discussion and writing

Who, then, should be cast in an August Wilson drama? Directors should assist actors as they explore this question and Wilson's position on color-blind casting. Hence, the second part of *Fences's* workshop should be a discussion about color-blind casting. Actors should respond to the following questions:

- Is Wilson's position on color-blind casting a valid one?
- Despite Wilson's position, should any actor, regardless of race or ethnicity, be allowed to portray a Wilsonian character?
- After reading Wilson's 'The Ground on Which I Stand' speech, I feel . . .
- How has reading *Fences* and the address effected my interpretation of the play and understanding of Wilson's dramatic vision?

The aim of these questions is to enable actors, especially non-African-American actors who may agree with Wilson, to discern the difference between reading the play within a classroom setting and a public performance. In an educational setting, students, actors and teachers should not shy away from 'performing' Wilson because they fear disrespecting his work. Instead, this type of setting affords all persons, regardless of race, the opportunity to experience the universality of Wilson's characters and their words. Moreover, allowing and encouraging students to 'become' Troy, Rose, Cory or Gabriel further accomplishes the goal of theatre that Wilson notes in 'The Ground on Which I Stand':

> Theater asserts that all of human life is universal. Love, Honor, Duty, Betrayal belong and pertain to every culture or race. The way they are acted out on the playing field may be different, but betrayal is betrayal whether you are a South Sea Islander, Mississippi farmer, or an English Baron. All of human life is universal, and it is theater that illuminates and confers upon the universal the ability to speak for all men. (Wilson, 1997: 503)

A professional production of *Fences*, however, launches a different discussion. Actors should revisit the questions posed in the previous discussion and writing section, with the additional question of does an actor, director and/or theatre company have a responsibility to honor a dramatist's casting desires? *Fences's* stage directions do not include the words '*the people in this play are black*' as did, for example, several of Ed Bullins's works, one of Wilson's dramatic influences. Yet, in 'The Ground on Which I Stand' and several interviews, Wilson clearly states his position, and despite this omission, he composed *Fences* about African-American characters and African-American culture.

Fences: performing the play

Actors should be asked to read *Fences* and Wilson's 'The Ground on Which I Stand' speech before attending the workshop, and keep a journal of questions and initial responses to the play (structure, stage directions), its characters, language and Wilson's address. The following questions may serve as response prompts:

- Which character would I most like to portray and why? What traits does this character possess?
- How does music work within this play?
- What is the theme of this work?
- What is the most intriguing line, monologue, or moment in the play?
- Do I see a relative or friend reflected in this play?
- What has changed from the play's beginning to the play's end?

The workshop should begin with a 30–45 minute discussion in which each actor summarizes his pre-workshop journal responses to the play, specifically focusing on the African-American culture that Wilson seeks to present and preserve in his works. After this discussion, the drama should be read act by act, with the actors reading the scenes first through their own cultural tones, attitudes and mannerisms, and then from Wilson's race-specific cultural perspective. This exercise should accomplish two things: (1) The actors will have the opportunity to test Wilson's color-blind casting assertion; and (2) The actors will begin to understand why Wilson is intent on upholding African-American cultural nuances and motifs. Following each scene, the actors should revisit the questions posed in the pre-workshop exercise and pose new questions about the play. (Note: A dry erase board set up during workshop will enable the actors to write down their questions for all to see and consider later.) At the workshop's end, the actors will leave with an expanded list of questions and responses to consider as they begin to better understand Wilson and *Fences*, and locate their theatrical selves within its pages.

A focus on character

After approaching *Fences* as a socio-historical work, actors should spend time working within the characters themselves. This approach asks that actors focus mainly on the character questions posed in the initial workshop, especially because *Fences* is Wilson's only character-driven play (the other nine works are more ensemble-focused). Also, this approach encourages students to locate both the specificity of the African-American male character and the humanity that enables these characters to be recognized and appreciated within any culture. The actors should also remain cognizant of Wilson's focus on realism. *Fences* is a realistic drama from beginning to end, and its characters must be portrayed in this way. Thus as the actors participate in the following exercises, they should always think of the characters as real human beings, not fictionalized stereotypes or figments of one's imagination.

Troy Maxson: the everyman

James Earl Jones immortalized the role of Troy Maxson at Yale and on Broadway, and offers an imperative piece of advice for the actor who will portray Troy or any other Wilsonian character: 'It's hard for an actor to go wrong if he's true to the words August Wilson has written' (Jones, 2001: 84). Troy's character should be played along with each character in the drama, individually and collectively. For example, the actors should pull out the scenes (see key scenes for suggestions) in which Troy participates in a one-on-one, or rather one-against-one dialogue with another character. The 'I am having an affair scene' between Troy and Rose, and 'the father–son battle' between Troy and Cory are two scenes that will demonstrate Troy's 'power' and the other characters' powers also, especially to be bold and strong enough to verbally and, in Cory's case, physically challenge Troy.

Actor Ron McCall, who portrayed Troy in the Houston, Texas-based Ensemble Theatre Company's 2002 production of *Fences*, tells interviewer Everett Evans that he followed Wilson's advice for portraying his characters: 'One thing August has taught me is that to do his plays effectively, you can't judge his characters. If you start off being too judgmental about their actions, you can't take the full journey with them' (Evans, 2002: 11). Hence, actors should visualize *Fences's* characters individually and without critique of their actions or statements so that they may forge a connection between the characters and themselves.

An interesting exercise centering on Troy's character is one where actors, both male and female, are asked to select one of Troy's speeches or stories, and recite it as if they were the Troy that they have visualized. Next, the actors should perform this same speech as the Troy whom they think Wilson created – a responsible, but flawed, black male survivor. This exercise will afford actors numerous opportunities to 'hear' and 'see' the different forms that Troy's character may take in comparison to the Wilsonian ideal for Troy. Additionally, this approach will enable female actors the opportunity to experience Troy's side of the story before enacting the role of Rose. Playing Rose after portraying Troy will allow the actors who read Rose's lines to understand what Rose means when she says that she allowed Troy's needs and wants to consume her, and admits that she is responsible for her actions.

After reading one of Troy's speeches or stories, consider the following explanation for his actions and words and compare it with your own reflections on the character.

Troy Maxson, just as does the play, sits on the cusp of change. Within his person are scars of his past and revolutionary inklings of the change that would come in the decade of the 1960s. Troy's grand stature and selfishness should be mixed with humor and confusion and, for the actor who assumes this role, demonstrated at all times on the stage. It should be remembered that Troy, like *Ma Rainey's* Levee, embodies the warrior, has survived homelessness, hunger, imprisonment, and attempted to be a responsible husband, father, and man. A former Negro League Baseball player, Troy should be portrayed as a competitor who, despite what others say, refuses to accept the fact that he is too old to play ball anymore. Instead, he creates a metaphorical baseball stadium from the materials of his life, and both plays in and umpires game after game until he finally strikes out.

Actors should then be asked the following questions:

- If Troy were an animal, what type of animal would he be?
- Is Troy a survivor?
- What is Troy's real character flaw?
- Is Troy a character that you, regardless of ethnicity or gender, empathize with?
- Do men like Troy exist in other cultures? What are their stories?
- Is Troy an everyman character?

Jim Bono: the friend

Jim Bono's character is the admitted follower in this drama. Bono's character is one that all of the actors should experience, for friendship, like many of *Fences's* themes, is a universal relation that most individuals experience at least once during their lifetimes.

The first exercise that the actors should participate in is one that has been used in numerous team building programs – the trust fall. The actors should be paired and given 5 minutes to discuss the concept of trust. Although the actors may not have met prior to this workshop, they should begin to think of themselves as members of a group or team who must trust and work together to offer a seamless production of the work. After this brief discussion, one actor in each pairing should be blindfolded. Once blindfolded, that actor should stand and reflect upon the devotion that Bono expresses toward Troy. Bono clearly believes that Troy is a good person; hence, Bono should also know that if he falls, Troy will catch him. This is the type of faith that the blindfolded actor should try to imitate as she prepares to continue this exercise. When mentally prepared, the blindfolded actor should simply fall back and the sighted actor should catch his partner before she hits the ground. This exercise should be repeated with the sighted actor now being blindfolded. Also, this exercise may be carried out with the entire group.

Although *Fences's* stage directions describe Bono as an admiring follower, actors should be careful not portray this as a weakness. Actors should consider the strength that is needed to try to follow a man like Troy. Moreover, actors should remember that Bono has experienced many of the same things – prison, inadequate housing, poverty, hard work, love – that Troy has, but he admires the manner in which Troy has met these challenges. Troy, then, is Bono's role model. The following exercise should enable actors to comprehend this point.

The role-modeling exercise asks actors to consider one actor or director whom they consider to be their artistic role model. Before the group, the actors should perform the character of their artistic role model. For example, the actor who selects James Earl Jones should recite the lines and act in the way that Jones has in any one of his stage or screen performances. After each actor has had the opportunity to role-play as his role model, the actors should think about how their role model would portray either Bono or one of the drama's other characters. Granted, this exercise does not focus upon friendship, but it focuses on admiration and imitation, both traits that Bono and Cory exhibit within the work.

Wilson's woman: playing Rose Maxson

Although in several interviews Wilson stated that women were not the primary focus of his work, at least his early work, Rose Maxson's powerful voice emerged early in his dramatic cycle the cycle and became a model for the female characters who would follow her. Stage and screen actress Mary Alice originated the role of Rose in a workshop at the Yale Repertory Theatre and carried it on through to Broadway. Alice was able to model Rose on the women in her family – her mother and grandmother – in order to create a character whose love for her family and honest assessment led to a character who was just as strong as Troy (Bennetts, 1987).

Rose's character should be carefully studied and understood by students who wish to play her. Just as Alice culled lessons from the female branches of her family tree, students should research and note the feminist struggles of their foremothers. For students who may not be able to locate a woman who in Rose's words accepted 'what life offered her as woman', I suggest that they examine histories and images of black women. Moreover, although Wilson already introduced the quintessential blues woman with the character Ma Rainey, and Rose is introduced approximately 20 years following the prominence of blues women, students should listen to recordings by female blues artists and read blues lyrics in order to understand Rose's lament, anger and ability to make Troy a 'womanless man' without leaving her home or her marriage.

After studying Rose and the histories of African-American women, actors should cull Rose's parts from the play text and use them as they visualize and contrast Rose of 1957 to a twenty-first-century Rose. Questions to consider:

- Does Rose still exist? How does she look, sound, act?
- How does she walk and stand?
- Are all women Rose? Is she vulnerable or strong?
- If Rose were an animal, which animal would she be?

Rose's character is a particularly ideal character to workshop inter-ethnically, for her character encompasses two American second-class citizens – African Americans and women. Actors should be encouraged to consider how Rose's powerful words and emotion may be part of the larger world of women, who in many cultures of the world have had to 'settle for [what] the world [had] offered them' as women. However, Rose's character as an African-American woman should also be fully considered, for in adherence to Wilson's vision, her African-Americanness further complicates her femaleness.

Actors should workshop Rose speaking from the perspectives of women from different eras, races, countries, educational and socio-economic levels. For example, how would Rose respond to Troy if she were a college-educated woman? Imagine a Rose and Troy who were West Indian? How would Rose sound and what cultural differences would be illustrated in her role? What if Rose were a descendant of the numerous Irish immigrants who settled in the Hill District? Lastly, actors should visualize and portray Rose during different eras in women's history and African-American history: 1890s, 1920s, 1930s, 1940s, 1970s, 1980s, and 2008, and ask if Rose would have been the same or different? If so, how and why?

Lyons Maxson: the musician
Lyons Maxson is *Fences's* outsider. While he is Troy's son and Cory's brother, he does not reflect Troy's influences as much as the other

characters do. Lyons is a jazz man; he performs and lives his life according to the chords of 'Chinese music', Troy's term for Lyons's chosen musical genre. Thus, he is a foreigner, at least in Troy's world, who crosses the borders into and out of the Maxson yard for the purpose of borrowing and repaying money from his biological father.

The actor who portrays Lyons needs to attempt to locate his center and motivation, and answer the question: how does Lyons measure up to Troy? One exercise that will enable an actor to begin to dissect Lyons's character is to first consider his name and imagine him possessing lion-like qualities. Is Lyons 'the king of the jungle'? Is he a skilled hunter? Is he a worthy opponent for his father? In order to begin to answer these questions, the actor should be paired with the actor portraying Troy and, using one of the key scenes discussed in Chapter 2, portray Lyons as if he were a human possessing lion-like characteristics. If this exercise is effective, the actor will see that Lyons is able to move to his own rhythm because he is both a visitor and the untamed kernel of Troy's psyche. Lyons and Troy are essentially one and the same, for they are determined to live according to their own mandates. Lyons's foreign or rather outsider status, however, has protected him from Troy's attempts to control and shape him as he does with Cory.

Cory Maxson: mirroring the father
Actor Courtney B. Vance starred in the role of Cory Maxson in both the Yale Repertory and Broadway productions. *New York Times* theatre critic Frank Rich applauded his portrayal of Troy's son/protégé and noted that Vance's portrayal of Cory provided the comparable strength needed when played against James Earl Jones's Troy. At the end of the play, Rose tells Cory that he is just like his father. Hence, actors should attempt to locate Troy inside of Cory and ask the question: despite their battles, how are they even more akin than biological father and son?

Actors should perform Cory as a mirror image of Troy. Through-out the play, Cory mimics Troy's actions, and, as Rose points out, he is more like his father than he knows. Thus, actors should stage Troy and Cory as 'twins'. Cory should posses Troy's walk, posture and some slight head tilt that not only illustrates the statement, 'like father, like son', but also illuminates the characteristics that these two warring characters share. The actor who portrays Cory should also remember that he is a man-child, Troy's man-child. A high-school senior, Cory is a young adult, but also the son of his domineering father. Thus, as he imitates Troy, his mimicry should be slightly adolescent and awkward. After the actor has mastered Troy's movements alone, the actors should workshop any of the scenes that feature Troy and Cory together. A powerful scene in which to stage this mirror image is the scene where Cory and Troy struggle for the bat, and then Cory is banished to the other side of the fence. Both actors should place their hands on the bat (they will be facing each other) and then take turns improvising what they would want to say to each other if they could.

Gabriel Maxson: the spectacle character

Gabriel Maxson is *Fences's* spectacle character. He has few lines but his movements (walk and posture), especially because he is a wounded war veteran, speak volumes about his character. Gabriel is a character who must be read and visualized both psychologically and physically. His character utilizes his entire person – externally and internally – as it conveys his belief in his brother's humanity and candidacy for heaven. Gabriel is a character whose subtle lessons are overshadowed by Troy's bold pronouncements. His independence is the core of his personality, but this is shrouded by his seeming mental handicap. In order to locate this aspect of Gabriel's charac-ter, actors are asked to identify a physical trait or movement (such as a limp, wink, whistle or hand gesture) or utilize a particular tone, dialect and volume for Gabriel's voice that could be his 'trademark'.

Once identified, the actors should merge Gabriel's word with his trademark and use them to enhance Gabriel's character and move him from the drama's periphery.

Actors should be careful to workshop Gabriel's character more in the light of a court jester and not an imbecile. Each actor, regardless of gender, should perform Gabriel's character so that they may understand how the drama's other characters react and respond to him. The first exercise asks that each actor attempts to 'become Gabriel'. Each actor should, based upon their interpretation of the character and script, role-play as if they were Gabriel, remembering that Gabriel is a wounded war veteran, an entrepreneur, a bachelor and a member of the Maxson family. The challenge will be for the actors to balance all of Gabriel's self-actualized characteristics with the reality of his illness – his belief that he is the Angel Gabriel. Gabriel's character should also be exercised with the words 'I AM A MAN' at the fore of each actor's mind, for Gabriel is as much a Maxson man as Troy is.

Actors should locate Gabriel's masculinity alongside of his disconnection from reality by speaking Gabriel's lines and insert the phrase 'I am a man' either at the beginning or at the end of the lines. By merging this phrase with the script, the actors should begin to uncover that despite his position in society and the Maxson family, Gabriel understands both who and what he is. A second exercise asks that the actors form pairs with one actor representing society and the other character portraying Gabriel. The actor portraying society should ask the actor portraying Gabriel questions and make comments to which Gabriel will respond simply 'I am a man'. The aim of this exercise is to challenge the actors to use this phrase as means to communicate a list of other responses and emotions such as: 'You have to recognize me', 'I am deserving of your kindness', 'I am not invisible', 'I exist' and 'I am sane'.

This last suggestion leads to the second exercise that actors should undertake when working with Gabriel's character. While Gabriel and Troy do not have the same type of conflicting relationship that Troy has with everyone else in his family, Gabriel and Troy are conflicting or rather contrasting parts of the same whole. Hence, this exercise requires that Gabriel's and Troy's dialogue be performed together, and that Gabriel's last words and actions be performed against one or more of Troy's stories or speeches. This exercise will reveal the differences between the brothers, but also remind the actors that despite their differences Troy and Gabriel are brothers who are the sons of an embittered sharecropping father. Thus, they share a familial legacy and a social and cultural history as black men in the 1950s. Moreover, contrasting these two characters further illumines the centrality of family and kinship in *Fences*; a kinship that will remain despite how much one family member hurts the others.

Fences: the setting

Mastering the language and the characteristics of *Fences's* characters is a vital component of a workshop. Yet, *Fences's* title and setting should also be workshopped as vital components of each character's persona and the drama's overall theme. In order to accomplish this a connection should be made between the setting's fence, porch, yard, and the Maxson home. The actors should discuss and visualize these inanimate objects as imperative structures in human being's lives. This exercise will require three actors working in tandem. One actor will be the fence, another the yard, and the third actor will portray either the Maxson's home or the home's porch. The group members should arrange themselves as their respective 'characters' – fence, yard and home or porch – and speak to one another about their relation to one another, especially as objects and places where humans interact. Because much of *Fences's* plot takes place in, on or around these spaces, the actors should familiarize themselves with these spaces and use this knowledge as they construct the characters' roles.

Conflicts and key scenes

Fences is riddled with conflicts. From its title on through its final scene, numerous opportunities for exploration of these conflicts arise. This section will offer suggestions for which conflicts and keys scenes should be explored within a workshop setting.

Fathers and sons

The conflict between Troy and Cory dominates the drama, but the most important scene that illustrates this conflict is the scene in which Cory is banished from his family's home. This scene is imperative to the drama's meaning, for it simultaneously illustrates Cory's exit from his father's home and into a world in which he can forge for himself. Moreover, this scene and exemplifies the meaning of the adage 'history repeats itself'. As this scene is workshopped, students must remain cognizant of the African-American male's struggle to parent in a world in which he is continuously forced to prove that he is a man, a citizen, a human being and also to believe it. The struggle between Cory and Troy in this scene builds from a look (a hard stare) into a verbal fisticuffs, and then into a struggle for the bat, an ironic symbol of baseball, the great American sport, and manhood in that it bears a strong resemblance to a phallus, the symbol of masculinity. Cory loses the bat at this scene's conclusion, and, as mentioned, is banished to the other side of the fence and outside of his house, but he should not exit this scene dejected or emasculated because he has lost the bat. Instead, he should leave his father's house disheveled, but confident that if he has become bold enough to challenge his father, he has become bold enough to challenge the world. He has become a man.

Fences provides an excellent opportunity for students to workshop conflicting dialogue, particularly exchanges between a husband and wife. The scenes between Troy and Rose run the gamut from being loving exchanges where Troy tells his tales and Rose chastises him for his lies and brashness, to lengthy and desperate explanations of

Troy's needs and Rose's sacrifices, and questions and statements concerning their daily lives. As students workshop any of these marital conflicts, they must be constantly aware of the state of the black family in 1957. Troy and Rose, on the one hand, have beaten the odds. Troy is employed as a garbage man, first a loader, and by the play's end a driver, and Rose is a homemaker. They own a home, have a son, and for all sakes and purposes are living within a nuclear family – the antithesis to the pervading stereotypical lives of many African-American families. They work from paycheck to paycheck and love one another as best they can. They have been a unit for 18 years and have lived as close to the American dream as America will allow. With this in mind, students should pay close attention to the meaning of marriage for the African-American culture, remembering that African-American slaves were not allowed to be legally joined, and that after emancipation and during the Reconstruction Period, many African Americans sought to make their unions legal as means to protect their family unit. For Rose marriage is sacred and important despite the sacrifice, so Troy's infidelity has done more than wound her; it has also wounded the idea of black marriage that she has desperately attempted to create for their family.

Two scenes focus on the Maxsons' marital discord. The first is when Troy announces his affair and impending fatherhood affair and Rose opens up about the truth of her standing next to him for 18 years (162, 163, 165). This scene is filled with rage, passion, tears, disillusionment and pain from both parties. It should be staged as a duet with the actors sharing the emotional language, but speaking different words. One way to workshop this scene is to have the actors sit facing one another and read the parts with only the script between them. A second exercise for this same scene places the actors on opposite sides of the stage, fence or porch. This way the distance between Troy's thoughts and Rose's thoughts is both verbal and visual, and creates a space where their differing perspectives collide and dissolve into the air. A third exercise would have Troy and Rose move up and down the porch's stairs as they speak their lines, trying to achieve their objectives, with Rose standing on the porch as her last 'stage'. This last exercise visualizes the discord between Troy and Rose, and allows Rose's character to have full attention as she counters Troy's arguments.

The second example of the Troy–Rose conflict should be rife with tension but also with compassion. Like its visual influence, Bearden's painting *Continuities*, Troy's standing in the yard with the baby in his arms should be staged as a dramatic representation of the actual collage, highlighted by the characters' words. During this scene, Troy's voice should be strong but he should falter at times and almost whisper when he addresses the infant in his arms. Rose's voice should now be the commanding and declarative one. As she speaks, her words should sound cold, distant and emit an indifference that has come from months of pent-up anger. Rose's final words in this scene are the most stinging and should be literally hurled at Troy as she takes the baby into her arms and walks away from him.

This scene should be workshopped using again a spatial hierarchy with Rose on the porch, her stage, and Troy in the yard, humbled and in a sense begging Rose through his fumbling cradling of the baby, Raynell, for her assistance. Rose possesses all of the power in this scene, and her role must present this. Her final words, which are some of the most memorable and powerful of all of Wilson's female characters, should be delivered with a tone of finality.

A second exercise asks that actors improvise and state what other things Rose and Troy might have said to each other in this scene. Actors should ponder what they think Troy wishes he could say or what they think he should say, then speak these lines. The actors portraying Rose should expand her few lines and state what they think she really feels in both her heart and soul, but refuses to state.

Friendship

Friendship is an important component of *Fences's* plot. The drama begins with the friends, Troy and Bono, entering the Maxson yard, and the drama concludes with Bono, along with Troy's family, in the Maxson yard preparing to bury his flawed hero, his friend. All of the actors involved in a production of *Fences* should recognize this illustration of male bonding, for it furthers Wilson's dogmatic desire to depict the struggles and survival of black men. By allowing Troy and Bono to be friends, especially with the hyper-masculine Troy telling his friend, 'I love you nigger' (152), Wilson challenges existing stereotypes about black men lacking the ability to love and bond with others.

Actors should test this theme by reflecting on the friendships that they have had and transfer those feelings into Troy's and Bono's relationship. Also, actors should improvise a scene in which Troy and Bono tell each other why they are friends, and why they value one another's friendship. Each actor should take turns saying one sentence that begins 'I value your friendship because __'. Another suggestion for this motif is to have actors physically demonstrate ways that men illustrate friendship through special handshakes, high-fives, coded language and/or gestures. Actors should be creative and challenge themselves to consider how men from various cultures physically demonstrate the friendship bond. The actors should work together in pairs to develop several different friendship techniques and present them to the group. This simple exercise will help to replicate, again, *Fences's* realism.

Motifs and ideas to explore

What makes a man?

As *Fences's* scholars and critics have noted, the play is a rites of passage drama. It is a work that centers upon the trials that, specifically, male characters must undergo before they can be crowned with the title 'man'. However, once all of *Fences's* rites of passage ceremonies have concluded, the question of what makes a man looms. Is a man a responsible being as Troy Maxson boasts that he is? Is a man a loving brute who rules his home with an iron fist? 'What is a man?' is the question that Troy struggled to answer because he had to assemble an image of manhood from scraps of masculinity shown to him by his estranged father and within a racist society that refused to see him as a man.

Legacy

Essential to understanding any of Wilson's dramas is the idea of legacy. When the cycle is read chronologically from *Gem of the Ocean*, to *Fences* at its center, on through *Radio Golf*, the question of legacy or inheritance (cultural inheritance) is as prominent as any of the characters in the work. Through their personas and accompanying stories, or rather songs, all of Wilson's characters share their legacies with their peers and their audiences, and invite them to evaluate their worth and meaning.

In *Fences*, the legacies offered are not all favorable. Troy offers and passes down a legacy of responsibility but not of love, of selfishness instead of selflessness, and of strength and perseverance instead of cowardice. Like the blues song 'Old Blue' that Cory and Raynell heard Troy sing during his lifetime, and that they perform as a duet on the day of Troy's funeral, Troy's legacy has been passed on, especially to Cory. However, just as the essence of an undocumented oral text may remain the same while the words change, Cory and Raynell will have the opportunity to examine their father's legacy, forgive him for its flaws, and build a newer and sin-less legacy. Wilson's prologue and Rose's words to Cory, fittingly, frame *Fences's* plot and enclose a story about love, patience, and most of all forgiveness.

The Wilsonian character

Lastly, any actor who has the opportunity to workshop an August Wilson play should heed the words of Wilsonian actor Charles Dutton. Twice I have heard Mr Dutton explain to audiences that every actor and every black actor cannot be a Wilsonian actor (Dutton, Charles, 2005 and 2007). Wilson's words are powerful and they motivate the plot and the characterizations and the actions of the play. Any actor who cannot embrace and respect the long story monologues and the survivalist perspectives of Wilson's characters need not attempt Wilson's work.

Hence, this last exercise asks that each actor attempt to locate and/or create the Wilsonian character within himself. As they study and memorize the drama's lines, they should be ever mindful of Wilson's characters' histories and experiences. Simply, place yourself, if you are willing, into the complexities of a culture and its people who have endured despite enslavement, disenfranchisement and segregation and learn from their strength. Finally, remember that the Wilsonian character is not a victim.

5 Conclusion

Fences is a wonderfully sound, African-American centered, universal drama peopled with extraordinary characters and motivated by a specific plot that vacillates between past legacies and future legacies; it is a drama that will find itself produced and studied well into the twenty-first century. Numerous productions and revivals of this seminal work continue to appear on American stages, thus proving the immortality of Wilson's dramatic vision and its protagonist, Troy Maxson.

The future of *Fences* is especially promising now that it has become the 'middle child' of Wilson's dramatic canon. Because Wilson completed the last play, *Radio Golf*, in his planned twentieth-century cycle before his death, now the dramas are often organized and presented chronologically. *Fences*, set in 1957, finds itself in the center of the cycle. This is a fitting position for the play because it is the work that illustrates the changing tides of American social and political structures, and the small victories that African Americans have achieved since the Emancipation Proclamation, the Reconstruction Period, and Jim Crow segregation policies. New productions of the work, such as The Kennedy Center's 2008 staged reading of the drama and the anticipated Broadway revival of the work that will be directed by Pulitzer Prize winning dramatist Suzan-Lori Parks, alongside Wilson's other plays, will now enable *Fences* to be read and viewed as the fifth chapter of the dramatic novel or fifth installment of Wilson's century-long chronicle play. This type of chronological staging of his works will afford audiences the opportunity to trace the evolution of the African-American culture through Wilson's characters and note that, despite the changing laws and tides, this culture and its people continue to fight for equality and wholeness intra- and inter-culturally.

In classrooms, Wilson's work is now moving from margin to centre as more scholars are finding ways to incorporate his works into departments outside of theatre, drama and literature. Students in history and sociology departments are being introduced to Wilson's plays as secondary sources (particularly *Fences* and *Joe Turner's Come and Gone*), so that they may develop a fuller understanding of the effects of racial discrimination on African Americans. These same disciplines also utilize Wilson's plays to further their teachings on African-American cultural motifs, especially the vernacular genres blues, folklore and storytelling. Thus Wilson's *Fences* is continuing to solidify its presence in academic circles and forging an interdisciplinary ground for study.

Presently, *Fences's* film adaptation has been delayed because of Paramount Picture's failure to meet Wilson's directorial terms, and I am not certain if this conflict will ever be resolved. However, if the Wilson estate and Paramount reach an agreement, this production will enable Wilson's *Fences*, like *The Piano Lesson*, to not only reach (and re-reach) numerous and diverse audiences, but it will also allow another great dramatic work to be immortalized beyond the page and stage. Moreover, this production may set the stage for more Wilsonian film adaptations to be made.

I would like to imagine a few future productions that could take the reception of *Fences* to new audiences and provoke new insights. *Fences* could be staged alongside its twin, *Death of a Salesman*. This type of coupled production of two of the most important American dramatic works of the twentieth century would enable actors and directors the opportunity to stretch their dramatic abilities from Milleresque to Wilsonian moments (or vice versa) and provide critics and scholars an opportunity continue to discuss the connections between these two American dramatists and their works.

Fences illustrates Troy Maxson's Northern and pre-Civil Rights Movement demand for equality within the sanitation industry. In 1968, 3 years after *Fences's* conclusion and Troy's demise, sanitation employees in Memphis, Tennessee, embarked on their own a strike protesting the accidental deaths of two of their fellow workers. This strike brought Martin Luther King, Jr to the city twice, where during his last visit he delivered the famous 'I Have a Dream' speech and was assassinated by a sniper's bullet. Because the sanitation workers and their representative slogan 'I Am a Man' echoes *Fences's* theme of Civil Rights and equality, this drama could be staged in Memphis, Tennessee, as part of the yearly commemoration of this event. I contend that a Memphis production would further elevate the Civil Rights characteristics dramatized in the play and prove that both Northern and Southern African Americans face(d) the same types of discrimination.

Lastly, *Fences* is a multilayered historical work that not only embodies the tenets of the Civil Rights movement, but it also personifies the great American sport, baseball. A future production of *Fences* could be staged on a baseball field, with the Maxson's home and yard centered within the baseball diamond. Baseball is Troy's metaphorical mission statement and life's philosophy; hence, I suggest that the metaphor be moved to the center of a production and used to further complicate the lives of an African-American everyman, and those of his family and friends, who must learn to interpret his language – baseball, strikes, steals, outs – so that they may understand his base, his life. The purposes of a fence around a baseball diamond are to keep those persons outside of the stadium safe from the ball and away from the action of the game, and to allow for proof of a home run. The purposes of *Fences*, the drama, are to offer a glance into African-American culture in the 1950s, prove that black life is human life, demonstrate Wilson's ability to write a structured, single-character focused drama, and most importantly, protect and preserve the integrity of black life, family, love and culture. Wilson's *Fences* reminds us that from a coal a diamond is formed; from the baseball diamond, Troy preaches his philosophical view.

Fences has numerous staging possibilities for the future. Now that the Wilsonian cycle of dramas is complete, directors and actors will conceive of new ways to link the works and the characters into entities that flow easily from one to another. Scholars and teachers will identify new pedagogical strategies through which to introduce Wilson to the next generations of Wilsonian actors, directors, scholars and teachers. In sum, any and each new production of Wilson's dramas will enable his work to cement his position within the American theatre as one of our greatest playwrights.

Timeline 1950–65

Year	Politics	Culture
1950	The United States entered the Korean War; The U.S. Supreme Court ruled that dining cars on interstate trains could not be segregated; Ralph Bunche wins the Nobel Peace Prize for his service as a U.N. mediator in Palestine	According to the U.S. Census, approximately 1.6 million African Americans had migrated from Southern states to Northern states; Gwendolyn Brooks became the first African-American author to win a Pulitzer Prize; Juanita Hall became the first African American to win a Tony award; Jackie Robinson became the first African American to appear on the cover of *Life* magazine; Pittsburgh, PA had a population of 676,806; the Hill District (August Wilson's home and *Fences'* setting) had a population of 20,813
1951	The U.S. Army disbanded the twenty-fourth Infantry Regiment unit	Roy Campanella was named the National League's Most Valuable Player
1952	The United States detonated the first Hydrogen Bomb at Eniwetok Atoll, located in the Pacific Ocean; for the	*Invisible Man*, written by Ralph Ellison, was published

Year	Politics	Culture
	first time in 71 years no known lynchings had taken in the United States; Dwight D. Eisenhower was elected to his first term as President of the United States	
1953	Dwight D. Eisenhower was sworn in as the thirty-fourth President of the United States; The Korean War officially ended on 27 July 1953	Ellison's *Invisible Man* won the National Book Award; Watson and Crick published their discovery of DNA (April); Louis Peterson's *Take a Giant Step* opened on Broadway; Larry Doby became the first African-American player in the American League when he signed with the Cleveland (Ohio) Indians
1954	The Brown vs. the Topeka Board of Education case resulted in the U.S. Supreme Court's decision to ban segregation in public schools	The New York Giants' Willie Mays was awarded the National League's Most Valuable Player title; Dorothy Dandridge starred in Otto Preminger's *Carmen Jones*
1955	The U.S. Interstate Commerce Commission banned segregation in Interstate travel facilities; The U.S. Supreme Court ordered all United States schools to begin desegregation plans	Montgomery, Alabama Bus Boycott begins following Rosa Parks's refusal to give up her seat at the front of the bus; 14-year-old Emmet Till was murdered
1956	President Dwight D. Eisenhower was elected to his second term as President	Singer Nat 'King' Cole became the first African American to host a television variety show

Year	Politics	Culture
	of the United States: The U.S. Supreme Court ruled that Montgomery, Alabama's bus segregation as unconstitutional	
1957	The Civil Rights Act of 1957 was passed to protect African-American voting rights; the Little Rock Nine, under the protection of U.S. Federal Troops, integrated Little Rock, Arkansas' Central High School; Ghana, West Africa became the first African nation to be decolonized	Tennis player Althea Gibson was the first African-American tennis champion at Wimbledon; Langston Hughes's *Simply Heaven* opened on Broadway; Baseball player Hank Aaron was named the National League's Most Valuable Player
1958	Clifford R. Wharton, Sr became the first African American to head an American Embassy in Europe. He became the minister to Romania	NASA, the North American Space Agency, was formed; Baseball player Ernie Banks was named the National League's Most Valuable Player; dancer Alvin Ailey founded the Alvin Ailey American Dance Theater
1959	Alaska became the forty-ninth state; Hawaii became the fiftieth state	Lorraine Hansberry's *A Raisin in the Sun* opened on Broadway. The play ran for 538 performances; Miles Davis released 'Kind of Blue'; Motown Records was founded in Detroit, Michigan by Barry Gordy; Jazz singer Ella Fitzgerald and band leader Count Basie became the first African Americans to win Grammy Awards

Year	Politics	Culture
1960	The Civil Rights Act of 1957 was strengthened by the Civil Rights Act of 1960 that was signed into law by President Eisenhower. This Act held the government more responsible when reviewing civil rights violations; The first televised American Presidential debate took place (John F. Kennedy and Richard M. Nixon)	Harper Lee's *To Kill A Mockingbird* was published
1961	John F. Kennedy became the thirty-fifth President of the United States; The U.S. ended diplomatic relations with Fidel Castro-led Cuba and supported the Bay of Pigs invasion	Kennedy established the Peace Corps; Alan Shepard became the first American to travel into space; Ossie Davis's play *Purlie Victorious*, opened on Broadway
1962	The United States government banned discrimination in public housing	Jackie Robinson became the first African American to be inducted into the Baseball Hall of Fame; the Negro Baseball League became defunct following the integration of American baseball
1963	Following the assassination of President John F. Kennedy, Lyndon B. Johnson became the thirty-sixth President of the United States on 22 November 1963	President John F. Kennedy was assassinated on 28 March 1963; over 250,000 people participated in the March in Washington; Rev. Martin Luther King, Jr delivered his seminal 'I Have a Dream' speech at the March in Washington; Sidney Poitier won the Oscar for Best Actor; Civil Rights Activist Medgar Evers was assassinated

Year	Politics	Culture
1964	The Civil Rights Act of 1964 was passed. This Act banned discrimination in public accommodations, employment and education; Lyndon B. Johnson was elected President of the United States; The twenty-fourth Amendment to the U.S. Constitution *abolished* a poll tax that was implemented to prevent Southern African Americans from voting	Dr Martin Luther King, Jr received the Nobel Peace; Cassius Clay (Muhammad Ali) won the Heavyweight Boxing Championship: Lorraine Hansberry's *The Sign in Sidney Brustein's Window* opened on Broadway
1965	The United States Congress passed the Voting Rights Act of 1965; The United States entered the Vietnam War; Thurgood Marshall was appointed solicitor general of the United States Supreme Court; Patricia R. Harris became the first African-American woman to be appointed a U.S. Ambassador (She was the Ambassador to Luxemburg.)	Malcolm X was assassinated; Satchel Paige was named the National Baseball Congress' All-time Outstanding Player; James Baldwin's *The Amen Corner* opened on Broadway

Further Reading

The play

August Wilson, *Fences*, in *August Wilson: Three Plays*, Pittsburgh: University of Pittsburgh Press, 1985 and 1991. The first edition of this play was published one year after its original Broadway opening. This edition is the final version of the drama as it was presented on Broadway.

The playwright

Bigsby, Christopher (ed.), *The Cambridge Companion to August Wilson*, Cambridge: Cambridge University Press, 2007. This collection of essays examines Wilson's life and career, his relationship to black theatre and the critical reception of his work, as well as including chapter-length studies of each play of his ten-play cycle by prominent Wilsonian scholars.

Bryer, Jackson R. and Mary C. Hartig, *Conversations with August Wilson*, Mississippi: University Press of Mississippi, 2006. The most definitive collection of Wilson's interviews from the beginning of his career in the 1980s up through the twenty-first century, this text enables Wilson scholars to read his perspectives first-hand.

Wilson, August, *The Ground on Which I Stand*, New York: Theatre Communications Group, 1996 and 2001. Offers an enlightening representation of Wilson's cultural-politics, his pride and allegiance to the African-American culture, and a call for all American theatre practitioners to work 'together' to create theatre spaces where all persons and cultures will be acknowledged and supported on their 'own ground', but also as part of American theatre.

Wilson, August, *A Conversation with August Wilson*, Producer and director Matteo Bellinelli; producer, Larry Adelman; writer Barbara Christian, San Francisco, CA: California News Reel, 1992. Using a montage of excerpts from Wilson's staged productions and photos and film footage from African-American history, this filmed interview introduces Wilson scholars to Wilson by way of his own words. In this interview, Wilson explains his Hill District youth, the influence of the blues on his work, and his concept of the 'blood's memory', that form of memory that is innate and that connects him and his characters with the memories and actions of their African and African-American pasts.

Wilson, August, *August Wilson: Writing and the Blues*, producer, Public Affairs Television, Inc., Princeton, NJ: Films for the Humanities, 1994. In this interview with Bill Moyers, Wilson walks through the Hill District and further explains his musical muse – the blues – and how Bessie Smith's 'Nobody Can Bake a Sweet Jelly Roll Like Mine' moved him and made him recognize a 'nobility' in the black voices that he heard growing up in the Pittsburgh Hill District. Wilson also discusses how his works are ways to enable African-American audiences to reconnect and recognize their Africanness.

The cultural context

Clark, Keith, *Black Manhood in James Baldwin, Ernest J. Gaines, and August Wilson,* Urbana: University of Illinois Press, 2002. A compelling discussion of representations of black manhood and masculinity, of particular interest to Wilson scholars is the chapter 'Race, Ritual, Reconnection, Reclamation: August Wilson and the Refiguration of the Male Dramatic Subject', which examines the manner in which Wilson constructs his African-American male characters 'to convey the multifaceted nature of post-1960s black male dramatic subjectivity' (101).

Hay, Samuel, *African–American Theatre: An Historical and Critical Analysis*, United Kingdom: Cambridge University Press, 1994. Offers a comprehensive overview of the development of African-American theatre from its beginnings up though the end of the twentieth century, including an important reading of Wilson's dramatic canon and its placement within the African-American theatrical continuum.

Lanctot, Neil, *Negro League Baseball: The Rise and Ruin of a Black Institution*, Pennsylvania: University of Pennsylvania Press, 2004. An in-depth study of the history of the American Negro League Baseball organization and its players, including important information about the cultural and economic responses that this league elicited.

Snodgrass, Mary Ellen, *August Wilson: A Literary Companion,* North Carolina: McFarland & Company Inc., 2004. Snodgrass offers an encyclopedia-styled explanation of August Wilson's plays, characters, settings, language and significant literary, sociological and historical terms used in scholarly and journalistic discussions of Wilson's works. This text also includes a detailed chronology of August Wilson's life and works from his birth in 1945 on through April 2005, and a genealogy chart of Wilson's family from his maternal grandmother to his daughter, Azula Carmen Wilson.

Williams, Dana and Sandra Shannon, *August Wilson and Black Aesthetics*, New York: Palgrave Macmillan, 2004. A collection of essays and interviews that explore the black aesthetic as presented in the works of August Wilson, including Harry

Elam Jr's 'August Wilson and Hip Hop' and Yolanda Williams Page's interview with Wilsonian actor Charles Dutton. This collection concludes with an insightful interview in which Wilson discusses his perspective on aesthetics.

Schwartzman, Myron, *Romare Bearden: His Life and Art*, New York: Harry N. Abrams, Inc., 1990. This compilation of Bearden's work, with a preface authored by August Wilson, visually and textually presents the works of Wilson's visual muse for *Fences*, *Joe Turner's Come and Gone* and *The Piano Lesson*.

Shannon, Sandra, *August Wilson's Fences: A Reference Guide*, Connecticut: Greenwood Press, 2003. The most definitive cultural and critical discussion of *Fences* as both a singular American classic and part of Wilson's ten-play cycle series, with informative material about Wilson's dramatic influences (especially artistic influences) and critical reception.

Websites

As of November 2007, when the words 'August Wilson's *Fences*' were typed into the www.google.com search engine, 620,000 sites appeared identifying everything from biographical timelines and interviews with Wilson and Wilsonian actors, to photos and playbills of productions of *Fences*. Hence, Wilson's legacy has been globalized by the World Wide Web. What follows are a few websites that offer specific information about Wilson and *Fences*.

'August Wilson', http://encarta.msn.com/media_461519498/August_Wilson.html. This site provides an excerpt from *Fences*, a photo of Wilson, and an audio file of Wilson reading Troy's discussion of death.

Ben Calvert and Nadine Warner, 'Study Guide for Court Theatre's Production of August Wilson's *Fences*'. http://www.courttheatre.org/

home/plays/0506/*Fences*/studyguide/*Fences*StudyGuide.pdf. This site offers a definitive exploration of *Fences*, beginning with Wilson's obituary and concluding with pre- and post-production topics and discussion questions.

'*Fences*', http://www.sparknotes.com/drama/Fences/. Spark notes offers a detailed discussion of the play's themes, characters, motifs and key facts. A quiz is also included.

'*Fences*', http://www.webenglishteacher.com/awilson.html. This site offers teachers and students lesson plans and assignments to use when teaching *Fences* and *The Piano Lesson*.

Portland Center Stage director Jonathan Wilson and cast, '*Fences* by August Wilson', http://www.youtube.com/watch?v=e1qov8jlkXQ. Members of the Portland Center Stage's production of *Fences* offer their insights on *Fences* and on portraying its various characters. This site provides wonderful insight that will supplement Chapter 4.

References

Note: All references to the play are to the 1985 edition of *Fences* found in *August Wilson: Three Plays*. Pittsburgh: University of Pittsburgh Press, 1991.

Awkward, Michael (1994), '"The Crookeds with the Straights": *Fences*, Race, and the Politics of Adaptation', in Alan Nadel (ed.), *May All Your Fences Have Gates: Essays on the Drama of August Wilson* (pp. 205–29). Iowa City: University of Iowa Press.

Bennetts, Leslie (1987), 'For Mary Alice, "*Fences*" Has a Universal Theme', 30 March 1987, *The New York Times* available at www.nytimes.com.

Blumenthal, Anna (2000), 'More Stories Than the Devil Go Sinners: Troy's Stories in August Wilson's *Fences*'. *American Drama* Vol. 9, Issue 2 (Spring): 74–96.

Booker, Margaret (1997), 'Building *Fences* in Beijing'. *American Theatre* (May/June): 50–52.

Cowan, Tom and Jack Maguire (1994), *Timelines of African-American History: 500 Years of Black Achievement* (pp. 215–51). New York: Perigee Books.

Creamer, Robert W. (1987), Rev. of '*Fences*'. *Sports Illustrated,* New York, 8 June 1987: 12–13.

Disch, Thomas (1987), 'Rev. of *Fences*'. *Nation,* 18 April 1987: 516–17.

Dutton, Charles (2005 and 2007), *Post-performance Discussion(s)*, Conference notes taken at the Conference 'Situating August Wilson in the Canon and the Curriculum' Two Day Symposium (8–9 April 2005) organized by Dr Sandra Shannon at Washington,

DC; and at Conference 'An August Wilson Celebration' at Rhodes College, (19–22 September 2007) organized by Rhodes College, Hattiloo Theatre, Memphis, TN; and The University of Memphis Performance, 19 September 2007, Memphis, TN.

Elam, Harry J. (2004), *The Past as Present in the Drama of August Wilson*. Michigan: The University of Michigan Press.

Ellison, Ralph (1964), *Shadow and Act*. New York: Random House.

Evans, Everett (2002), '"Fences" role liberating actor says'. *The Houston Chronicle* (Houston, Texas), 17 February 2002: 11.

Gerard, Jeremy (1987), 'Waterford to Broadway: Well-traveled "Fences"', *The New York Times*, 9 April 1987, available at www. newyorktimes.com.

Gittleson, Gia (2006), 'Angela Bassett (dialogue with Angela Basset)'. *Los Angeles Magazine* Vol. 51, Issue 9 (September): 230.

Greenberg, James (1991). 'Did Hollywood Sit on *Fences*?' *The New York Times*, 27 January 1991, available at www.nytimes.com.

Henry, William III (1987), '*Fences*'. *Time* 129 (6 April 1987): 81.

Herrington, Joan (1998), *I Ain't Sorry for Nothin' I Done: August Wilson's Playwrighting Process*. New York: Limelight.

Hughes, Langston (1925, 1959), 'I, Too, Am American', in Nellie McKay and Henry L. Gates, Jr (eds), *The Norton Anthology of African-American Literature* (Second edition) (P. 1295). New York: Norton, 2004.

Jones, James Earl (2001), 'Playwright: August Wilson'. *Time* 9 July 2001: 84.

Locke, Alain (1925), 'The New Negro', in Nellie McKay and Henry L. Gates, Jr (eds), *The Norton Anthology of African-American Literature* (pp. 960–70). New York: Norton, 2004.

Lyons, Bonnie (1997), 'An Interview with August Wilson', in Jackson Bryer and Mary Hartig (eds), *Conversations with August Wilson* (pp. 204–22). Mississippi: The University Press of Mississippi, 2006.

McDonough, Carla J. (1997), 'August Wilson: Performing Black Masculinity', *Staging Masculinity: Male Identity in Contemporary American Drama* (pp. 133–59). North Carolina: McFarland & Company, Inc.

Menson-Furr, L. (2005), 'Conference notes', taken at the Conference 'Situating August Wilson in the Canon and the Curriculum' two day symposium (8–9 April 2005) organized by Dr Sandra Shannon at Howard University, Washington, DC.

Moyers, Bill (1988), 'August Wilson: Playwright', in Jackson Bryer and Mary Hartig (eds), *Conversations with August Wilson* (pp. 61–80). Mississippi: The University Press of Mississippi, 2006.

Mulekwa, Charles (2005). www.earthtimes.org.

Nadel, Alan (1994), 'Boundaries, Logistics, and Identity: The Property of Metaphor in *Fences* and *Joe Turner's Come and Gone*', in Alan Nadel (ed.), *May All Your Fences Have Gates: Essays on the Drama of August Wilson* (pp. 86–104). Iowa City: University of Iowa Press.

Novice, Kevin, (2006), 'A Landmark Event in the American Theatre: Playhouse Announces Casting for *Fences* Revival', 7 July 2006 (press release): 1–2. www.pasadenaplayhouse.org.

Pereira, Kim (1995), '*Fences*: The Sins of the Father . . .', *August Wilson and the African-American Odyssey* (pp. 35–53). Illinois: The University Press of Illinois Press.

Pettengill, Richard (1993), 'The Historical Perspective: An Interview with August Wilson', Jackson Bryer and Mary Hartig (eds), *Conversations with August Wilson* (pp. 155–71). Mississippi: The University Press of Mississippi, 2006.

Pittsburgh Neighborhood Alliance (1977), *Pittsburgh Neighborhood Atlas: The Hill.* Pittsburgh: Pittsburgh Neighborhood Alliance.

Plimpton, George and Bonnie Lyons (1999), 'The Art of Theater: August Wilson'. *The Paris Review*, Vol. 41, no. 153: 1–28.

Rich, Frank (1985), 'Wilson's "Fences"'. *New York Times* 7 May 1985 (Tuesday). www.nytimes.com.

Richards, Lloyd (1985), 'Introduction' to *Fences*. New York: Plume (Penguin Group) 1986.

Rosen, Carl (1996), 'August Wilson: Bard of the Blues', in Jackson Bryer and Mary Hartig (eds), *Conversations with August Wilson* (pp. 188–203). Mississippi: The University Press of Mississippi, 2006.

Savran, David (1987), 'August Wilson', in Jackson Bryer and Mary Hartig (eds), *Conversations with August Wilson* (pp. 19–37). Mississippi: The University Press of Mississippi, 2006.

Shannon, Sandra (1991), 'August Wilson Explains His Dramatic Vision: An Interview', in Jackson Bryer and Mary Hartig (eds.) *Conversations with August Wilson* (pp. 118–54). Mississippi: The University Press of Mississippi, 2006.

Shannon, Sandra (1993), '"Blues, History, and Dramaturgy": An Interview with August Wilson'. *African-American Review* Vol. 27, No. 4: 539–59.

Shannon, Sandra (1995), 'Developing Character: *Fences*', *The Dramatic Vision of August Wilson* (pp. 89–117). Washington, DC: Howard University Press.

Shaw, Marc E. (2007), '*Fences*', in *Theatre Journal* Vol. 59, Issue (2): 282–84.

Simonson, Robert (2005), 'Sail Away: Wilson's *Gem of the Ocean* Ends Brief Broadway Run February 6' www.playbill.com 6 February 2005.

Snodgrass, Mary Ellen, (2004), *August Wilson: A Literary Companion*, North Carolina: McFarland & Company Inc.

'Stage View: The Year's Best; Engaged Drama Treated Real Concerns'. *The New York Times,* 27 December 1987. www.nytimes.com.

Staples, Brent (1987), '*Fences*: No Barrier to Emotion'. *The New York Times*, 5 April 1987. www.nytimes.com.

Verini, Robert (2006), '*Fences* stands tall in evocative revival', *Variety* Vol. 404, Issue 4 (September 11): 61.

Watlington, Dennis, (1989), 'Hurdling *Fences*', in Jackson Bryer and Mary Hartig (eds), *Conversations with August Wilson* (pp. 81–89). Mississippi: The University Press of Mississippi, 2006.

Werner, Craig (1994), 'August Wilson's Burden: The Function of Neoclassical Jazz', in Alan Nadel (ed.), *May All Your Fences Have Gates: Essays on the Drama of August Wilson* (pp. 21–50). Iowa City: University of Iowa Press.

Williams, Dana and Sandra Shannon (2004), 'A Conversation with August Wilson', *August Wilson and Black Aesthetics* (pp. 187–95). New York: Palgrave.

Wilson, August (1985), *Fences*, in *August Wilson Three Plays* (pp. 95–192). Pittsburgh: University of Pittsburgh Press, 1991.

Wilson, August (1990), Foreword, in Myron Schwartzman's *Romare Bearden: His Life and Art*. New York: Harry N. Abrams.

Wilson, August (1992), *Two Trains Running*. New York: Plume, 1993.

Wilson, August (1994), 'I Want a Black Director', in Alan Nadel (ed.) *May All Your Fences Have Gates: Essays on the Drama of August Wilson* (pp. 200–4). Iowa City: University of Iowa Press.

Wilson, August (1997), 'The Ground on Which I Stand'. *Callaloo* Vol. 20 No. 3 (Summer): 493–503.

Wolfe, Peter (1999), 'Introduction: From Street to State' and 'The House of Maxson', *August Wilson Stories* (pp. 1–22 and 55–75). New York: Twayne Publishers.

Index

—